$300 + 80 + 15 =$ ☐

$500 + 30 + 14 =$ ☐

$900 + 70 + 11 =$ ☐

$400 + 120 + 8 =$ ☐

$600 + 140 + 9 =$ ☐

$500 + 120 =$ ☐

$100 + 160 + 11 =$ ☐

$200 + 130 + 14 =$ ☐

$500 + 170 + 10 =$ ☐

$600 +$ ☐ $+ 13 = 653$

$300 +$ ☐ $+ 18 = 378$

$400 +$ ☐ $+ 16 = 516$

$200 +$ ☐ $+ 14 = 334$

$600 + 50 +$ ☐ $= 668$

$200 + 70 +$ ☐ $= 289$

$400 + 60 +$ ☐ $= 470$

$$\begin{array}{r} 800 \\ 80 \\ +\ 13 \\ \end{array}$$

$$\begin{array}{r} 400 \\ 60 \\ +\ 14 \\ \end{array}$$

$$\begin{array}{r} 700 \\ 50 \\ +\ 17 \\ \end{array}$$

$$\begin{array}{r} 600 \\ 140 \\ +\ 18 \\ \end{array}$$

$$\begin{array}{r} 400 \\ 130 \\ +\ 13 \\ \end{array}$$

$$\begin{array}{r} 300 \\ 40 \\ +\ \\ \hline 358 \\ \end{array}$$

$$\begin{array}{r} 800 \\ 130 \\ +\ \\ \hline 945 \\ \end{array}$$

Ref: *Lab Sheet Annotations*, pages 63 and 75.

•••••• D-23

Name _____ Date _____

(300   +   40   +   6)
- (200   +   10   +   4)
(100   +   30   +   2)

$$\begin{array}{r} 346 \\ -214 \\ \hline 132 \end{array}$$

Short way

(700   +   80   +   9)
- (400   +   30   +   3)
(+   +   )   _____

Short way

(600   +   180   +   9)
- (400   +   90   +   3)
(+   +   )   _____

Short way

(700   +   150   +   7)
- (500   +   70   +   4)
(+   +   )   _____

Short way

(800   +   40   +   13)
- (200   +   20   +   8)
(+   +   )   _____

Short way

(500   +   100   +   6)
- (300   +   20   +   6)
(+   +   )   _____

Ref: *Lab Sheet Annotations*, page 63.

Name _____

Date _____

Short way
(800 + 100 + 4)
- (400 + 60 + 2)
( ) + ( ) + ( )

Short way
(700 + 90 + 10)
- (100 + 40 + 8)
( ) + ( ) + ( )

Short way
(600 + 90 + 10)
- (500 + 10 + 3)
( ) + ( ) + ( )

Short way
(700 + 50 + 17)
- (200 + 40 + 9)
( ) + ( ) + ( )

Short way
(600 + 30 + 14)
- (100 + 20 + 8)
( ) + ( ) + ( )

Short way
(900 + 10 + 0)
- (300 + 10 + 0)
( ) + ( ) + ( )

Short way
365
- 233

You write the long way.
( ) + ( ) + ( )
- ( ) + ( ) + ( )
( ) + ( ) + ( )

Short way
479
- 171

You write the long way.
( ) + ( ) + ( )
- ( ) + ( ) + ( )
( ) + ( ) + ( )

Ref: *Lab Sheet Annotations*, page 63.

Name _____ Date _____

$435 = 400 + 30 + \boxed{}$

$435 = 400 + 20 + \boxed{}$

$435 = 300 + \boxed{} + 5$

$435 = 300 + \boxed{} + 15$

$362 = 300 + \boxed{} + 2$

$ = 300 + \boxed{} + 12$

$ = 200 + 160 + \boxed{}$

$ = 200 + 150 + \boxed{}$

$711 = \boxed{} + 10 + 1$

$ = \boxed{} + 0 + 11$

$ = \boxed{} + 110 + 1$

$ = \boxed{} + 100 + 11$

$888 = 8h + \boxed{}t + 8u$

$ = 8h + \boxed{}t + 18u$

$ = \boxed{}h + 18t + 8u$

$ = 7h + 17t + \boxed{}u$

Ref: *Lab Sheet Annotations*, pages 63 and 75.

Name _____ Date _____

h	=	hundreds
t	=	tens
u	=	units

7h + 5t + 11u = [761]

9h + 6t + 14u = [ ]

3h + 4t + 17u = [ ]

7t + 19u = [ ]

3h + 0t + 12u = [ ]

7h + 14t + 0u = [ ]

8h + 16t + 0u = [ ]

4h + 10t = [ ]

5h + 15t = [ ]

6h + 10t = [ ]

4h + 10t = [ ]

9h + 10t = [ ]

4h + 10t + 3u = [ ]

5h + 10t + 7u = [ ]

3h + 10t + 1u = [ ]

8h + 15t + 1u = [ ]

6h + 13t + 8u = [ ]

3h + 17t + 5u = [ ]

2h + 19t + 6u = [ ]

14t + 3u = [ ]

6h + 9t + 10u = [ ]

7h + 9t + 10u = [ ]

3h + 9t + 10u = [ ]

3h + 10t + 10u = [ ]

5h + 10t + 10u = [ ]

7h + 11t + 10u = [ ]

6h + 14t + 12u = [ ]

3h + 17t + 15u = [ ]

8h + 15t + 14u = [ ]

3h + 13t + 14u = [ ]

6h + 16t + 17u = [ ]

8h + 18t + 19u = [ ]

8h + 17u = [ ]

4h + 12u = [ ]

Ref: *Lab Sheet Annotations*, pages 63 and 75.

●●●●●●● D-27

five hundred thirty-two 532

h	t	u			
5	(3)	2	500 + ☐ + 2 = 532
4		2	400 + ☐ + 2 = 532
5		12	500 + ☐ + 12 = 532
4		12	400 + ☐ + 12 = 532

six hundred fifty 650

h	t	u			
6	5	(0)	600 + 50 + ☐ = 650
5	15		500 + 150 + ☐ = 650
6	4		600 + 40 + ☐ = 650
5	14		500 + 140 + ☐ = 650

four hundred five 405

h	t	u
	0	5
	10	5
3		5
3		15

seven hundred thirty-six 736

h	t	u
	3	6
6		6
7	2	
6		16

six hundred 600

h	t	u
6		0
	10	0
5		0
5	9	

Ref: *Lab Sheet Annotations*, pages 63 and 75.

Name _____

Date _____

	hundreds	tens	units	
A				In this row are: $2_h + 4_t + 3_u$ _____ They equal _____
B				In this row are: h t u _____ They equal _____
C				In this row are: h t u _____ They equal _____
D				In this row are: h t u _____ They equal _____

Do lab sheet D-30 next.

Ref: *Lab Sheet Annotations*, pages 64 and 77.

Name _____   Date _____

The chart on the left shows the ways for regrouping 243 as shown on lab sheet D-29. For each of the subtraction problems below, choose the best regrouping from the chart. Study the example.

	□	▭	⬜	·
A	2	4	3	
B	1	14	3	
C	2	3	13	
D	1	13	13	

Example — Which is best? A B (C) D   — C gives me enough units

```
 h  t  u
    2  13
 2  4  3
-1  2  5
--------
 1  1  8
```

Problems:

```
 h  t  u          A B C D
 2  4 (3)
-1  3  6
```

```
 h  t  u          A B C D
 2  4 (3)
-   6  7
```

```
 h  t  u          A B (C) D
 2  4 (3)
-1  0  9
```

```
 h  t  u          A B C D
 2  4 (3)
-1  7  1
```

```
 h  t  u          (A) B C D
 2  4  3
-1  2  2
```

```
 h  t  u          A B C D
 2 (4) 3
-   9  3
```

```
 h  t  u   Which is best?   A (B) C D
 2 (4) 3
-1  5  1
```

```
 h  t  u          A B C D
 2  4 (3)
-1  2  7
```

Ref: *Lab Sheet Annotations*, pages 64 and 77.

●●●●●● D-30

hundreds	tens	units	

O

In this row are:

h	t	u

They equal _____.

P

In this row are:

h	t	u

They equal _____.

Q

In this row are:

h	t	u

They equal _____.

R

In this row are:

h	t	u

They equal _____.

Do lab sheet D-32 next.

Ref: *Lab Sheet Annotations*, pages 64 and 77.

Name _____

Date _____

Write in the chart the regroupings of 465
that are on lab sheet D-31. Use them to do
the subtraction problems on this page.

h	t	u
O		
P		
Q		
R		

O
P
Q
R

h	t	u

$$\begin{array}{r} 465 \\ -\ \ 75 \\ \hline \end{array}$$

$$\begin{array}{r} 465 \\ -343 \\ \hline \end{array}$$

$$\begin{array}{r} 465 \\ -439 \\ \hline \end{array}$$

$$\begin{array}{r} 465 \\ -207 \\ \hline \end{array}$$

$$\begin{array}{r} 465 \\ -\ \ 73 \\ \hline \end{array}$$

$$\begin{array}{r} 465 \\ -288 \\ \hline \end{array}$$

$$\begin{array}{r} 465 \\ -324 \\ \hline \end{array}$$

$$\begin{array}{r} 465 \\ -\ \ 58 \\ \hline \end{array}$$

$$\begin{array}{r} 465 \\ -\ \ 92 \\ \hline \end{array}$$

$$\begin{array}{r} 465 \\ -161 \\ \hline \end{array}$$

$$\begin{array}{r} 465 \\ -434 \\ \hline \end{array}$$

Ref: *Lab Sheet Annotations*, pages 64 and 77.

••••••D-32

Name_____ Date_____

	hundreds	tens	units

h t u
| 3 | 2 | 4 |

300

20

+   4

324

3 hundreds   2 tens   4 units

Color:

h t u
| 3 | 1 | 14 |

Add: 300
        10
     + 14

Color:

h t u
| 2 | 12 | 4 |

Add:

Color:

h t u
| 2 | 11 | 14 |

Add:

Ref: *Lab Sheet Annotations*, pages 64.

Name_____ Date_____

hundreds	tens	units	

S			Color:
			
			h t u
			`2` `7` `0`
			
			Add: 200
			      70
			     + 0

T			Color: h t u `1` `17` `0` Add:
U			Color: h t u `2` `6` `10` Add:
V			Color: h t u `1` `16` `10` Add:

Ref: *Lab Sheet Annotations*, pages 64.

Subtract 451 from 527.

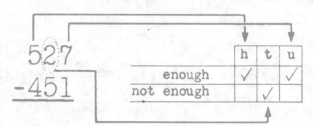

527
−451

	h	t	u
enough	✓		✓
not enough		✓	

h	t	u
4	12	7

−4 5 1

7 6

	h	t	u
enough	✓	✓	✓
not enough			

h	t	u

−4 5 1

	h	t	u
enough			
not enough			

Subtract 317 from 724.

724
−317

	h	t	u
enough			
not enough			

h	t	u

−3 1 7

	h	t	u
enough			
not enough			

h	t	u

−3 1 7

	h	t	u
enough			
not enough			

Subtract 327 from 678.

678
−327

	h	t	u
enough			
not enough			

h	t	u

−3 2 7

	h	t	u
enough			
not enough			

h	t	u

−3 2 7

	h	t	u
enough			
not enough			

Subtract 539 from 921.

921
−539

	h	t	u
enough			
not enough			

h	t	u

−5 3 9

	h	t	u
enough			
not enough			

h	t	u

−5 3 9

	h	t	u
enough			
not enough			

Ref: *Lab Sheet Annotations,* pages 64 and 78.

●●●●●●● D-35

Name_____   Date_____

Subtract 320 from 600.

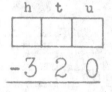

```
 600
-320
```

	h	t	u
enough			
not enough			

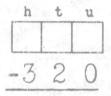

```
-3 2 0
```

	h	t	u
enough			
not enough			

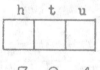

```
-3 2 0
```

	h	t	u
enough			
not enough			

Subtract 245 from 800.

```
 800
-245
```

	h	t	u
enough			
not enough			

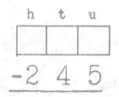

```
-2 4 5
```

	h	t	u
enough			
not enough			

```
-2 4 5
```

	h	t	u
enough			
not enough			

Subtract 304 from 700.

```
 700
-304
```

	h	t	u
enough			
not enough			

```
-3 0 4
```

	h	t	u
enough			
not enough			

```
-3 0 4
```

	h	t	u
enough			
not enough			

Subtract 165 from 402.

```
 402
-165
```

	h	t	u
enough			
not enough			

```
-1 6 5
```

	h	t	u
enough			
not enough			

```
-1 6 5
```

	h	t	u
enough			
not enough			

Ref: *Lab Sheet Annotations*, pages 64.

●●●●●● D-36

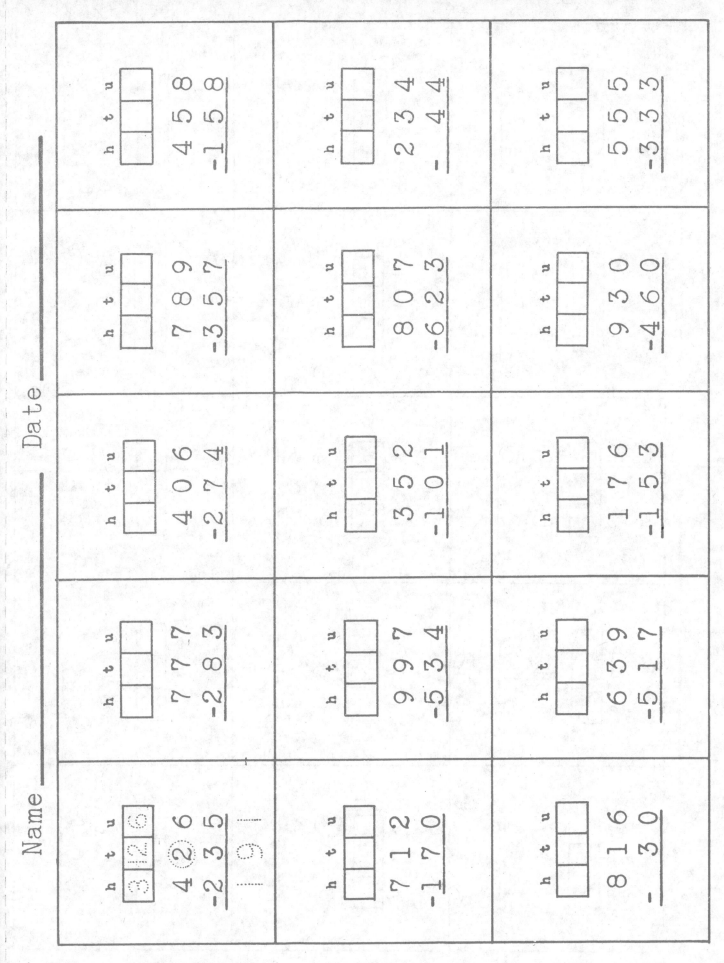

Ref: *Lab Sheet Annotations*, pages 64 and 78.

h t u	h t u	h t u
830 −417	786 −629	684 −408
969 − 78	803 −350	309 −264
583 −236	934 − 92	448 −236
784 −350	606 −275	890 − 96
337 −164	293 −160	532 −307

Ref: *Lab Sheet Annotations*, pages 64.

•••••• D-38

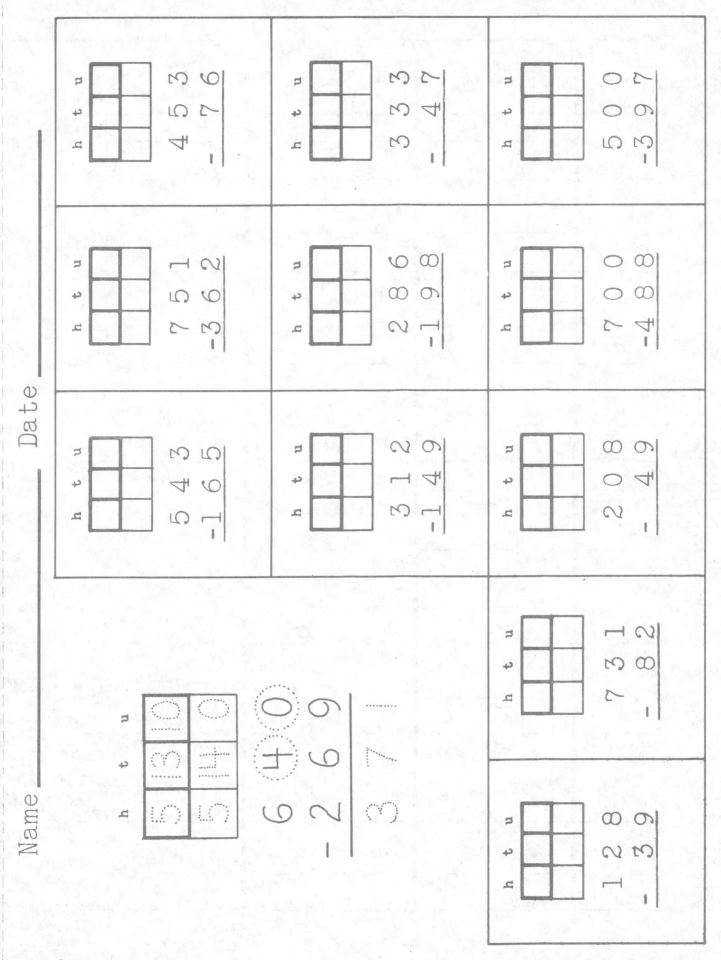

Name

Date

Ref: *Lab Sheet Annotations*, pages 64.

••••••• D-39

simple numeral	one ten exchanged for ten units			one hundred exchanged for ten tens			one hundred and one ten exchanged		
	h	t	u	h	t	u	h	t	u
357	3	4	17	2	15	7	2	14	17
520									
452									
460									
939									
754									
222									
800									
◯									

800	245	235	915	709
-311	- 67	-128	-726	-524

518	598	754	91	28
-329	-286	-555	-57	-25

605	780	59	777	70
-513	-684	-22	-688	-59

380	707	700	150	215
- 98	-686	- 49	- 20	- 19

Ref: *Lab Sheet Annotations*, page 64.

47	83	789	111	91
-35	-57	-691	- 37	-70

136	358	921	564	996
- 27	-264	-777	-313	-347

479	830	396	692	372
-385	-658	-163	-567	-281

700	593	346	589	503
-374	-241	-237	-395	-294

Ref: *Lab Sheet Annotations*, page 64.   •••••• D-42

My Red Book II

365 −220	849 −409	637 −537
17 − 8	170 − 80	27 −18
27 − 8	270 − 80	270 −180

Name _____

Date _____

-fold here-

444 −222	635 −617	408 −408
710 −107	483 −400	827 − 97
642 −151	839 −398	299 −201
683 − 95	720 − 84	835 −657

Ref: *Lab Sheet Annotations*, page 81.

●●●●●● D-43

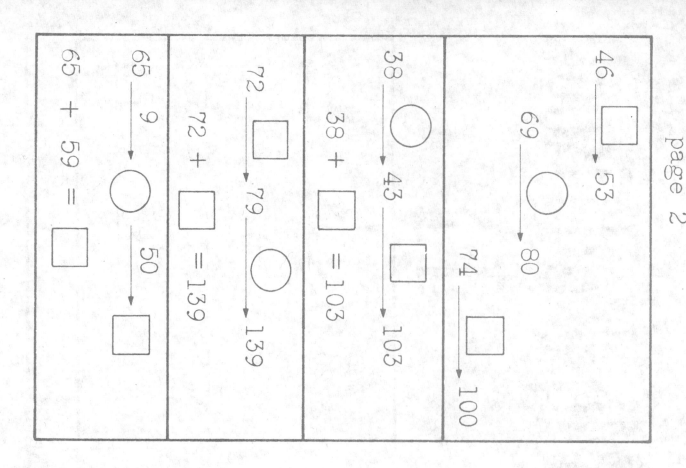

46 $\longrightarrow$ 53 □

69 $\longrightarrow$ 80 ○

74 $\longrightarrow$ 100 □

38 $\longrightarrow$ 43 ○

38 $\longrightarrow$ 103 □

38 + □ = 103

72 $\longrightarrow$ 79 □

72 $\longrightarrow$ 139 ○

72 + □ = 139

65 $\longrightarrow$ 9 ○

65 $\longrightarrow$ 50 □

65 + 59 = □

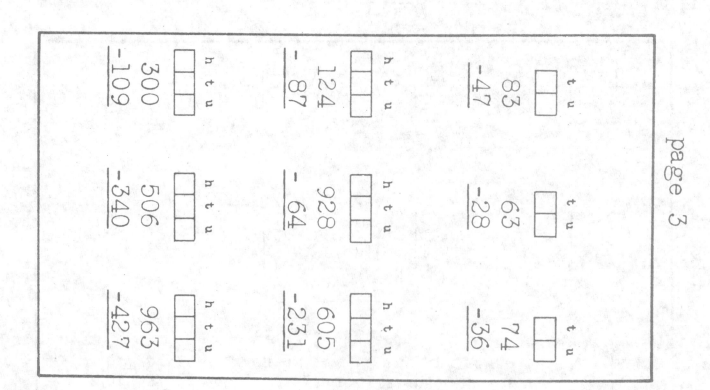

```
 t u
  8 3
- 4 7
```

```
 t u
  6 3
- 2 8
```

```
 t u
  7 4
- 3 6
```

```
 h t u
  1 2 4
 -  8 7
```

```
 h t u
  9 2 8
 -  6 4
```

```
 h t u
  6 0 5
 -2 3 1
```

```
 h t u
  3 0 0
 -1 0 9
```

```
 h t u
  5 0 6
 -3 4 0
```

```
 h t u
  9 6 3
 -4 2 7
```

Ref: *Lab Sheet Annotations*, page 81.

●●●●●● D-44

50	41	62	33	74	25	86
17	98	9	49	40	61	32
73	24	85	16	97	8	48
39	60	31	72	23	84	15
96	7	47	38	59	30	71
22	83	14	95	6	46	37

How to make your own practice problems:

1. Cut out the numeral squares.

2. Put them all in an envelope.

3. Take two squares out of the envelope and write the two numbers on a piece of paper.

4. Find the sum of these two numbers.

5. Find their difference.

6. Pick two other numbers from the envelope and do the same thing.

LOOK AT THE PICTURES ON THE NEXT LAB SHEET IF YOU DON'T UNDERSTAND.

Ref: *Lab Sheet Annotations*, page 104.   •••••• E-54

538	259	766	100	238	345	888
472	643	804	510	789	901	777
325	591	317	300	456	890	555
154	620	692	800	123	567	678
345	642	765	987	321	135	911
543	754	876	109	159	333	214

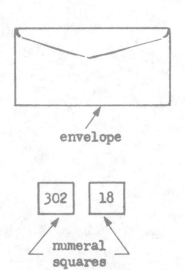

envelope

302   18

numeral
squares

Name _____   Date _____

○ 302   302
 + 18   − 18

      18   43
○ + 43   − 18

     165   165
○ + 59   − 59

your own
lab sheet

Ref: *Lab Sheet Annotations*, page 104.

●●●●●● E-55

Name _____ Date _____

Secret Code Arithmetic

Find the answer for each problem. Then
write the answer in code. If you have
no mistakes, you will have a message.

Code:
0 = l
1 = t
2 = h
3 = n
4 = i
5 = k
6 = o
7 = w
8 = s
9 = e

$$\begin{array}{r} 133 \\ -129 \\ \hline \end{array}$$

$$\begin{array}{r} 11402 \\ + 1033 \\ \hline \end{array}$$

$$\begin{array}{r} 3\frac{1}{2} \\ + \frac{1}{2} \\ \hline \end{array}$$

$$\begin{array}{r} 4340 \\ +1027 \\ \hline \end{array}$$

$$\begin{array}{r} 70 \\ -29 \\ \hline \end{array}$$

$$\begin{array}{r} 6666 \\ +1234 \\ \hline \end{array}$$

$$\begin{array}{r} 13 \\ - 9 \\ \hline \end{array}$$

$$\begin{array}{r} 1000 \\ - 101 \\ \hline \end{array}$$

$$\begin{array}{r} 199 \\ + 68 \\ \hline \end{array}$$

$$\begin{array}{r} 140 \\ - 99 \\ \hline \end{array}$$

$$\begin{array}{r} 2241 \\ +5690 \\ \hline \end{array}$$

The Message

____ ____ ____ ____

____ ____ . ____ ____

____ ____ ____ .

Ref: *Lab Sheet Annotations*, page 105.

Another Secret Code Message

Code:
0 = e
1 = n
2 = m
3 = b
4 = g
5 = s
6 = t
7 = o
8 = d
9 = i

```
 100        105       4780
-  4       - 10       -  2
```

```
  75         51         87
-  8        - 4        -20
```

```
 315         80       7000
-  7        - 9       -  80
```

Another Secret Code Message

Code:
0 = u
1 = i
2 = w
3 = h
4 = o
5 = a
6 = t
7 = f
8 = n
9 = s

```
 1224     909     8859      51
+1132    -201    -2540     -32
```

```
 1000     110     4103
- 158    - 16    + 5345
```

Ref: *Lab Sheet Annotations*, page 105.

6 × 21 = (6 × ☐) + (6 × ⬡) = ◯

4 × 18 = (4 × ☐) + (4 × ⬡) = ◯

7 × 15 = (7 × ☐) + (7 × ⬡) = ◯

4 × 34 = (4 × ☐) + (4 × ⬡) = ◯

5 × 23 = (5 × ☐) + (5 × ⬡) = ◯

9 × 105 = (9 × ☐) + (9 × ⬡) = ◯

4 × 42 = (☐ × 2) + (⬡ × 40) = ◯

6 × 27 = (☐ × 7) + (⬡ × 20) = ◯

3 × 82 = (☐ × 80) + (⬡ × 2) = ◯

```
    2 3              3 6              2 7
  × 4              × 3              × 4
  ─────            ─────            ─────
    1 2  (4 × 3)     1 8  (3 × 6)
  + 8 0  (4 × 20)  +      (3 × 30)  +
  ─────            ─────            ─────
    9 2
```

```
      24              28              53
   ×   5           ×   3           ×   6
      20
     100
     120
```

```
   41              63              57              52
 ×  8           ×   2           ×   3           ×   8
```

```
   33              44              18              15
 ×  5           ×   7           ×   6           ×   9
```

```
   17              48              26              54
 ×  7           ×   3           ×   6           ×   6
```

```
  205             330             236
 ×   4           ×   5           ×   3
```

```
  100          101          110          111
X   3        X   3        X   3        X   3


  200          202          220          222
X   4        X   4        X   4        X   4


  200          203          210          213
X   6        X   6        X   6        X   6


  300          308          330          338
X   3        X   3        X   3        X   3


  200          209          250          259
X   5        X   5        X   5        X   5


  400          403          440          443
X   2        X   2        X   2        X   2
```

Add the same number for each dot.

Add the same number for each line.

Fill the correct numerals in the frames below.

---

    (200) (200) (200) (200)

    (9) (9) (9) (9)

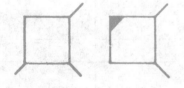   (18) (209)

These double boxes go with the pattern above.
Try to figure them out.

 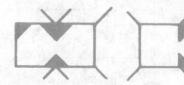 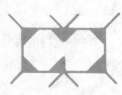

page 4

fold here

MON. TUE. WED.

$$28 \times 4 \qquad 33 \times 5 \qquad 64 \times 3$$

$$54 \times 6 \qquad 72 \times 7 \qquad 18 \times 0$$

$$47 \times 6 \qquad 39 \times 9 \qquad 45 \times 8$$

Name_____

Date_____

My Blue Book III

page 1

$3 \times 9 = \square$ $9 \times 3 = \square$

$6 \times 4 = \square$ $8 \times 3 = \square$

$7 \times 4 = \square$ $\square = 6 \times 5$

$9 \times \square = 36$ $\square = 5 \times 7$

$16 = \square \times \square$ $32 = \bigcirc \times \square$

$(3 \times 4) + (3 \times 7) = 3 \times \square$ $\square = \bigcirc$

$6 \times 10 + 6 \times 2 = 6 \times \square = \bigcirc$

$4 \times 10 + 4 \times 4 = \square \times 14 = \bigcirc$

$9 \times 10 + 9 \times 3 = 9 \times \bigcirc = \square$

$7 \times 10 + 7 \times 5 = 7 \times \bigcirc = \square$

$5 \times 16 = 5 \times \square + 5 \times 6 = \bigcirc$

$3 \times 18 = 3 \times 8 + 3 \times 10 = \square$

$8 \times 18 = 8 \times \square + 8 \times 10 = \bigcirc$

$5 \times 14 = \bigcirc \qquad 7 \times 13 = \bigcirc$

$4 \times 17 = \square \qquad 10 \times 19 = \square$

8 ×2	7 ×2	9 ×2	3 ×2
8 ×4	7 ×4	9 ×4	13 ×4
8 ×8	7 ×8	9 ×8	13 ×8

×	4	5	6	7
8				
3				
9				

Name _____

Date _____

Put ⬭ around the other names for $3\frac{1}{2}$.

Put ▭ around the other names for $2\frac{2}{3}$.

$7 \div 2$

$6 \overline{)16}$

$\frac{9}{2} + \frac{1}{2}$

$\left(3\frac{1}{2}\right)$

$\frac{14}{4}$

$\frac{8}{8} + \frac{8}{8} + \frac{8}{8} + \frac{4}{8}$

$\frac{7}{2}$

$8 \div 3$

$\frac{8}{3}$

$8 \overline{)28}$

$3 \overline{)8}$

$2 \overline{)7}$

$\frac{3}{3} + \frac{3}{3} + \frac{2}{3}$

$\boxed{2\frac{2}{3}}$

$\frac{6}{6} + \frac{6}{6} + \frac{4}{6}$

$\frac{2}{2} + \frac{2}{2} + \frac{2}{2} + \frac{1}{2}$

Name _____ Date _____

 red balls  green balls 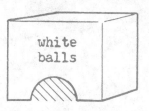 white balls

3 balls			Draw the red balls.	Draw the green balls.	Draw the white balls.
red	green	white			
$\frac{1}{3}$	$\frac{1}{3}$	$\frac{1}{3}$			
of them	of them	of them			

6 balls			Draw the red balls.	Draw the green balls.	Draw the white balls.
red	green	white			
$\frac{1}{3}$	$\frac{1}{3}$	$\frac{1}{3}$			
of them	of them	of them			

8 balls			Draw the red balls.	Draw the green balls.	Draw the white balls.
red	green	white			
$\frac{1}{2}$	$\frac{1}{4}$	the rest			
of them	of them	of them			

4 balls			Draw the red balls.	Draw the green balls.	Draw the white balls.
red	green	white			
$\frac{1}{4}$	$\frac{1}{4}$	the rest			
of them	of them	of them			

9 balls			Draw the red balls.	Draw the green balls.	Draw the white balls.
red	green	white			
$\frac{2}{9}$	$\frac{1}{3}$	the rest			
of them	of them	of them			

Now look at all the balls. How many are there?

___ are red,   ___ are green,   ___ are white.
30   30   30

$\frac{1}{3}$ of all the balls are

red
white
green
● ● ● ● ● ●   H-58

Name _____

Date _____

My
GREEN
BOOK II

Find the names for 2

$2 \times \frac{9}{9}$

$\frac{6}{12}$

$\frac{4}{4}$

$\frac{10}{5}$

$\frac{1}{4} + \frac{1}{2} + \frac{1}{2} + \frac{1}{4}$

$1 \div 2$

(2)

$\frac{2}{2} + \frac{2}{2}$

$\frac{98}{49}$

$2\frac{1}{2} - \frac{1}{2}$

$2 \div 1$

$1 \div \frac{1}{2}$

page 1

----------fold here----------

apples in a bowl

You get half as many
apples as mother.
You get twice as many
apples as baby.
Put your apples on
this plate.

page 4

Ref: *Lab Sheet Annotations*, page 162.

Use $<$, $=$, $>$ to make true sentences.

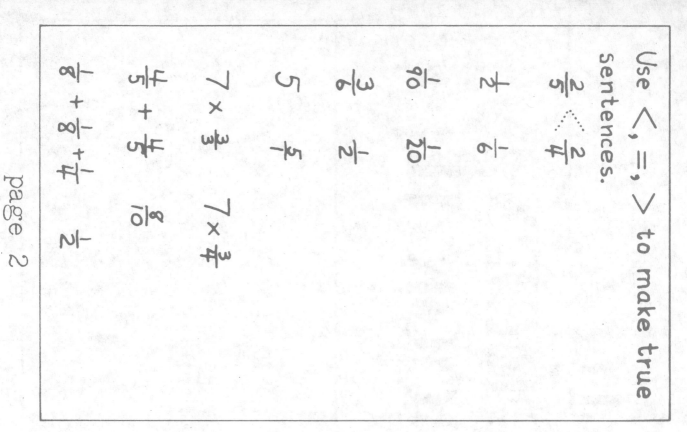

$$\frac{2}{5} \quad \frac{2}{4}$$

$$\frac{1}{2} \quad \frac{1}{6}$$

$$\frac{1}{90} \quad \frac{1}{20}$$

$$\frac{3}{6} \quad \frac{1}{2}$$

$$5 \quad \frac{5}{1}$$

$$7 \times \frac{3}{3} \quad 7 \times \frac{3}{4}$$

$$\frac{4}{5} + \frac{4}{5} \quad \frac{8}{10}$$

$$\frac{1}{8} + \frac{1}{8} + \frac{1}{4} \quad \frac{1}{2}$$

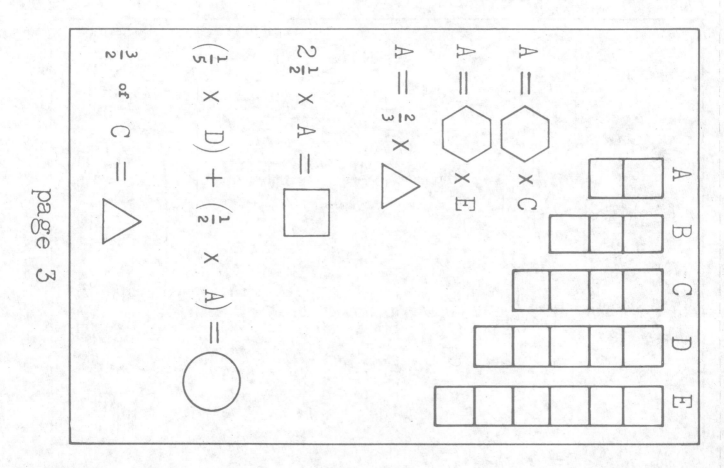

A = ⬡ × C

A = ⬡ × E

$A = \frac{2}{3} \times \triangle$

$2\frac{1}{2} \times A = \square$

$\left(\frac{1}{5} \times D\right) + \left(\frac{1}{2} \times A\right) = \bigcirc$

$\frac{3}{2}$ of C = $\triangle$

Ref: *Lab Sheet Annotations*, page 162.

●●●●●●●H-60

Name _____

Date _____

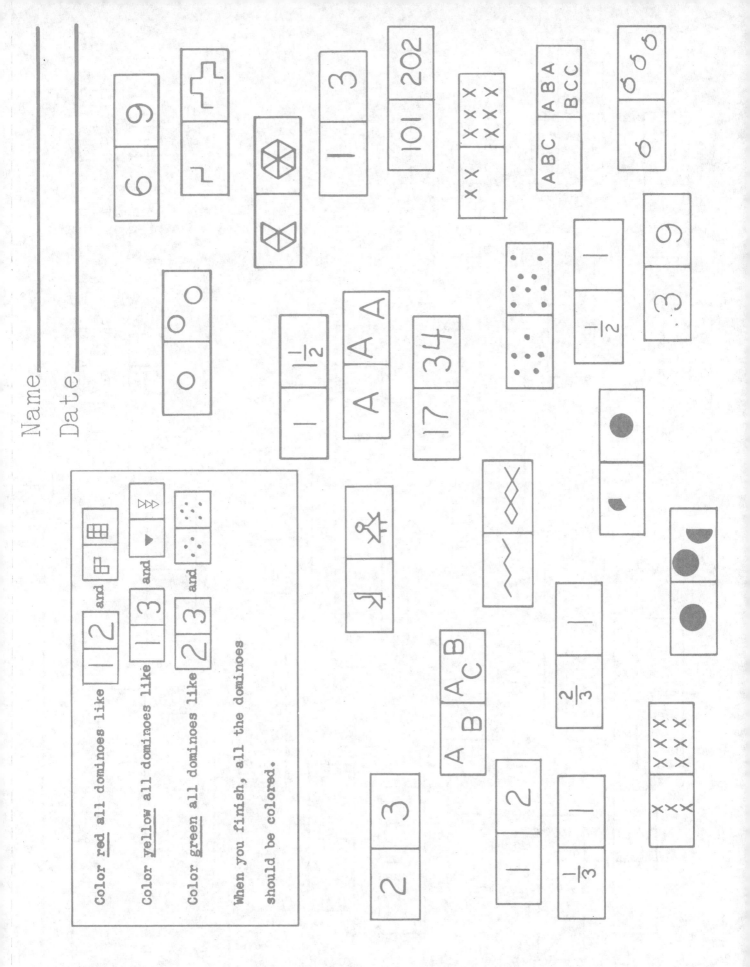

Color red all dominoes like ▢1▢2 and ▦▦

Color yellow all dominoes like ▢1▢3 and ▷▷▷ ▶

Color green all dominoes like ▢2▢3 and ⋮ ⋮

When you finish, all the dominoes should be colored.

Ref: *Lab Sheet Annotations*, page 164.

••••••• H-61

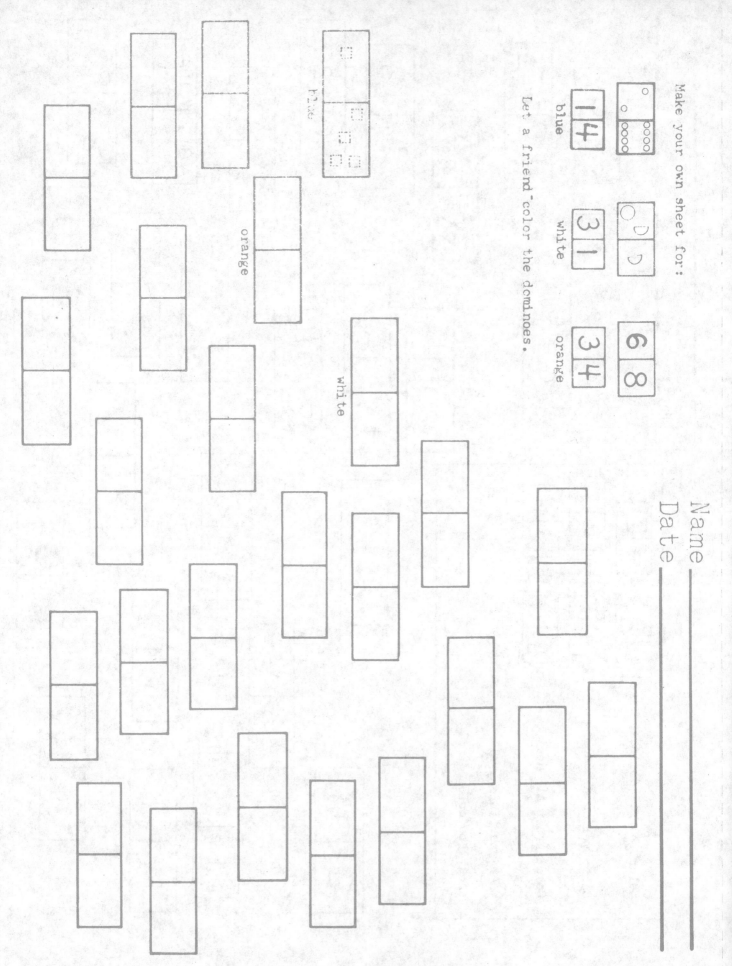

Make your own sheet for:

1 4	3 1	3 4
blue	white	orange

Let a friend color the dominoes.

orange

white

blue

Name _____

Date _____

Ref: *Lab Sheet Annotations*, page 164.

 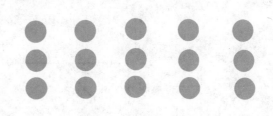 

$\frac{3}{5}$ of the marbles belong to Bill.

The other marbles belong to Nina.

How many marbles belong to Bill?

☐ marbles

How many marbles belong to Nina?

☐ marbles

 Two children stand on a scale at the same time.

The scale points to 50 kilograms.

One child weighs $\frac{3}{5}$ of 50 kilograms.

How many kilograms does the other child weigh?

☐ kilograms

Ref: *Lab Sheet Annotations*, page 165.

Name_____ Date_____

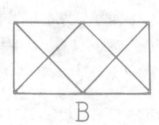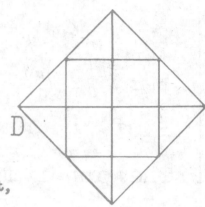

C . E A B D

If C is the unit,

then A = |.|.

    E =

    B =

    D =

If E is the unit,

then A =

    C =

    D =

    B =

If A is the unit,

then B =

    D =

    E =

    C =

If D is the unit,

then C =

    E =

    A =

    B =

If B is the unit,

then A =

    C =

    E =

    D =

2C = ☐

E + 2C = ☐

A + E + 2C = ☐

B + A + E + 2C = ☐

B + 2A + 3E + 8C = ☐

Ref: *Lab Sheet Annotations*, page 165.

●●●●●●●H-64

Name_____ Date_____

Try to do these division problems by thinking

of the steps you followed on lab sheets J-24, J-25, and J-26.

$12\overline{)168}$ think: $12\overline{)120+48}$ with $10 + 4$ above   write: $12\overline{)168}$ with 14 above

---

$9\overline{)99}$ $9\overline{)135}$ $6\overline{)90}$ $8\overline{)128}$

$4\overline{)96}$ $2\overline{)86}$ $3\overline{)81}$ $5\overline{)105}$

$11\overline{)121}$ $14\overline{)154}$ $4\overline{)128}$ $6\overline{)78}$

$3\overline{)156}$ $20\overline{)240}$ $40\overline{)240}$ $80\overline{)240}$

$\dfrac{150}{5} = \boxed{}$ $\dfrac{84}{4} = \boxed{}$ $\dfrac{64}{4} = \boxed{}$

$\dfrac{52}{2} = \boxed{}$ $\dfrac{96}{8} = \boxed{}$ $\dfrac{330}{10} = \boxed{}$

Study each picture. Then finish the problem.

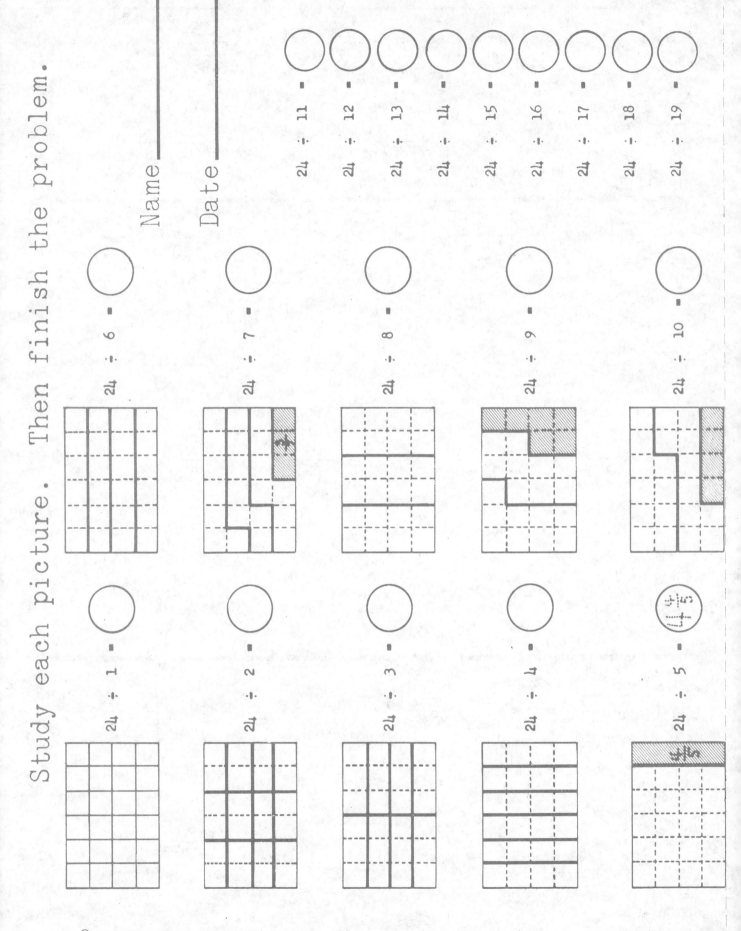

Name _____

Date _____

24 ÷ 11 = ○
24 ÷ 12 = ○
24 ÷ 13 = ○
24 ÷ 14 = ○
24 ÷ 15 = ○
24 ÷ 16 = ○
24 ÷ 17 = ○
24 ÷ 18 = ○
24 ÷ 19 = ○

24 ÷ 6 = ○
24 ÷ 7 = ○
24 ÷ 8 = ○
24 ÷ 9 = ○
24 ÷ 10 = ○

24 ÷ 1 = ○
24 ÷ 2 = ○
24 ÷ 3 = ○
24 ÷ 4 = ○
24 ÷ 5 = ○

Ref: *Lab Sheet Annotations*, page 184.

Name_____ Date_____

Rod pattern for 12

$12 \div 1 =$

$12 \div 2 =$

$12 \div 3 =$

$12 \div 4 =$

$12 \div 5 = 2\frac{2}{5}$

$12 \div 6 =$

$12 \div 7 =$

$12 \div 8 =$

$12 \div 9 =$

$12 \div 10 =$

$12 \div 11 =$

$12 \div 12 =$

Make a rod pattern for 15 and answer the following questions

$15 \div 1 =$

$15 \div 2 =$

$15 \div 3 =$

$15 \div 4 =$

$15 \div 5 =$

$15 \div 6 =$

$15 \div 7 =$

$15 \div 8 =$

$15 \div 9 =$

$15 \div 10 =$

$15 \div 11 =$

$15 \div 12 =$

$15 \div 13 =$

$15 \div 14 =$

$15 \div 15 =$

Make yourself a rod pattern for another number and answer the following questions:

☐ $\div 1 =$

☐ $\div 2 =$

☐ $\div 3 =$

☐ $\div 4 =$

☐ $\div 5 =$

☐ $\div 6 =$

☐ $\div 7 =$

and so on

Ref: *Lab Sheet Annotations*, page 184.

$$5\overline{)50} \quad\quad\quad\quad 10$$

$$5\overline{)5} \quad\quad\quad\quad 1$$

$$5\overline{)3} \quad\quad\quad\quad \tfrac{3}{5}$$

$$5\overline{)50 + 5 + 3} \quad 10 + 1 + \tfrac{3}{5}$$

$$5\overline{)58} \quad\quad\quad\quad 11\tfrac{3}{5}$$

$$8\overline{)80}$$

$$8\overline{)8}$$

$$8\overline{)2}$$

$$8\overline{)80 + 8 + 2}$$

$$8\overline{)90}$$

$$6\overline{)60} \quad\quad 7\overline{)70} \quad\quad 4\overline{)160}$$

$$6\overline{)30} \quad\quad 7\overline{)28} \quad\quad 4\overline{)20}$$

$$6\overline{)5} \quad\quad 7\overline{)3} \quad\quad 4\overline{)1}$$

$$6\overline{)60 + 30 + 5} \quad 7\overline{)70 + 28 + 3} \quad 4\overline{)160 + 20 + 1}$$

$$6\overline{)95} \quad\quad 7\overline{)101} \quad\quad 4\overline{)181}$$

Ref: *Lab Sheet Annotations*, page 184.

●●●●●●●J-30

$43 \div 10 = \bigcirc$

$\bigcirc \times 10 = 43$

$91 \div 9 = \bigcirc$

$\bigcirc \times 9 = 91$

$37 \div 7 = \bigcirc$

$\bigcirc \times 7 = 37$

$27 \div 9 = \bigcirc$

$\bigcirc \times 9 = 27$

$30 \div 8 = \bigcirc$

$\bigcirc \times 8 = 30$

Make up your own problems.

$5 \overline{)28}$ $6 \overline{)28}$ $7 \overline{)28}$ $8 \overline{)28}$

$5 \times \boxed{} = 28$ $7 \times \boxed{} = 28$

$6 \times \boxed{} = 28$ $8 \times \boxed{} = 28$

Ref: *Lab Sheet Annotations*, page 184.

Which numbers can be divided by ⑤
without a remainder?   (circle them)

35   39   60   72   45   43   82   66

Which numbers can be divided by ③
without a remainder?

14   22   27   18   13   33   42   60

Which numbers can be divided by ⑧
without a remainder?

24   58   48   70   19   32   36   56

Which numbers can be divided by ⑥
without a remainder?

26   42   38   48   20   30   54   72

Which numbers can be divided by ⑨
without a remainder?

17   29   61   80   35   84   27   73

Ref: *Lab Sheet Annotations*, pages 184 and 185.   ●●●●●● J-32

Try to find two ways to make FALSE.

$$\square + \square + 6 = 6 + \square + 5$$
$$\square + \square + 6 = 6 + \square + 5$$

$$3 \times \square = 2 \times \triangle$$
$$3 \times \square = 2 \times \triangle$$

$$19 - \square + 8 = 19$$
$$19 - \square + 8 = 19$$

$$\square + \square + \square + \square = \triangle + \triangle + \triangle$$
$$\square + \square + \square + \square = \triangle + \triangle + \triangle$$

Try to find two ways to make TRUE.

$$\square + \square + 6 = 6 + \square + 5$$
$$\square + \square + 6 = 6 + \square + 5$$

$$3 \times \square = 2 \times \triangle$$
$$3 \times \square = 2 \times \triangle$$

$$19 - \square + 8 = 19$$
$$19 - \square + 8 = 19$$

$$\square + \square + \square + \square = \triangle + \triangle + \triangle$$
$$\square + \square + \square + \square = \triangle + \triangle + \triangle$$

Ref: *Lab Sheet Annotations*, page 208.

••••••••L-21

Make these sentences <u>TRUE.</u>

$$\square - 80 = 80 - \square$$

$$60 - \square = \square - 60$$

Make these sentences <u>FALSE.</u>

$$\square + \square \neq \square$$

$$\square \times \square \neq \square$$

Make these sentences <u>TRUE.</u>

$$4 + \square + 2 = \square + \square$$

$$\square \times \square \times \square = \square$$

Make these sentences <u>FALSE.</u>

$$9 + \square = 12$$

$$8 + 13 > \boxed{}$$

Ref: *Lab Sheet Annotations*, page 208.

Name_____ Date_____

>, = , or <

$100 \div 3$

$2 \times 2 \times 2 \times 2 \times 2$

⬭

3×11

$4 \times 8\frac{1}{8}$

$8^2 \div 2$

$(5 \times 6) + 3$

⬭

$17 \div \frac{1}{2}$

33

>

=

Ref: *Lab Sheet Annotations*, page 209.

•••••••L-23

$>, =,$ OR $<$

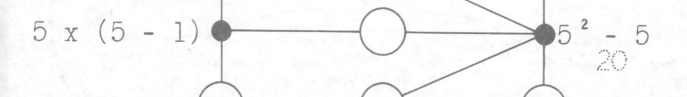

$(3^2 - 1^2) \times 3$ $(3 - 1)^2 \times 3$
24   12

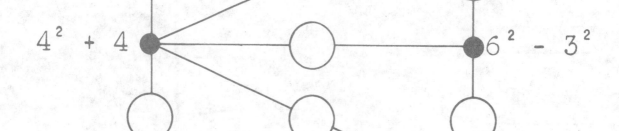

$5 \times (5 - 1)$ $5^2 - 5$
                       20

$4^2 + 4$ $6^2 - 3^2$

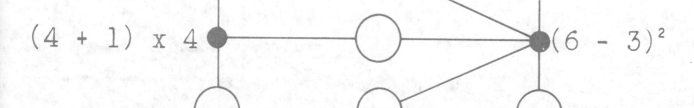

$(4 + 1) \times 4$ $(6 - 3)^2$

$1 \times 2 \times 3 \times 4$ $1^2 + 2^2 + 3^2$

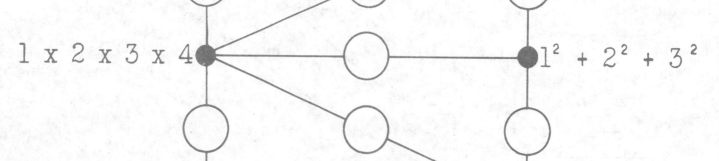

$(1 \times 2 \times 3)^2$ $(1 + 2 + 3)^2$

Ref: *Lab Sheet Annotations*, page 209.

Name_____ Date_____

Beans, Bags, Boxes

a bean   a bag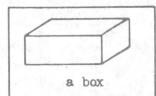
                           a box

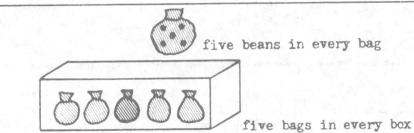

five beans in every bag

five bags in every box

boxes	bags	beans
	🛍	● ●
	🛍 🛍	●
▭		
▭	🛍 🛍 🛍	● ●
	4 bags	3 beans
2 boxes	0 bags	4 beans
3	0	0
3	2	2

Find the beans.

→ [ ] beans
→ [ ] beans
→ [ ] beans
→ [ ] beans
→ [ ] beans
→ [ ] beans
→ [ ] beans
→ [ ] beans

Hide the beans.

9 beans →			
20 beans →			
21 beans →			
22 beans →			
28 beans →			
24 beans →			
25 beans →			
26 beans →			
124 beans →			

Ref: *Lab Sheet Annotations*, page 221.

Supermarket Dairy Shelf

Buy:	2 gal.	1 gal.	½ gal.	1 qt.	1 pt.	1 c.
17 cups		1	◌	◌	◌	1
11 cups						
4 cups				1	◌	◌
15 cups						
16 cups						
40 cups						
29 cups						
31 cups						
32 cups						
51 cups						
⬡ cups	1	1	1	1	1	1
⬡ cups		1	0	0	1	1
⬡ cups		1	1	1	0	0
⬡ cups	1	0	1	0	1	0

Ref: *Lab Sheet Annotations*, page 221.

••••••M-22

Name	Date			
These are sugar lumps.	1 block	1 flat	1 long	1 unit
5 units in the least number of pieces.			⦂	2
9 units in the least number of pieces.				
6 units				
12 units				
16 units				
19 units				
22 units				
27 units				
26 units				
	1	0	0	1
	1	1	0	0
	1	1	2	0
	2	0	1	0
			2	2
	2	2	2	2

Ref: *Lab Sheet Annotations*, page 223.

●●●●●●M-23

9000 - 99   8901

                                                 8999

9000 - 909   8909

9000 - 990   8990

9000 - 109   8919

                                                 8891

one less than 9000   8991

ten less than 9000   8091

                                                 8010

eleven less than 9000   889

eleven less than 900   8989

101 less than 9000   8900

                                                 8890

110 less than 9000   8891

1000 less than 9000---------------------------8000

Ref: *Lab Sheet Annotations*, page 223.   ● ● ● ● ● ●M-24

Name _____ Date _____

Fill in the frames to make true sentences.

$5^2 - \boxed{9} = 4^2$ $\qquad$ $2^2 - 1^2 = \boxed{}$

$100 - 81 = \boxed{}$ $\qquad$ $7^2 + \boxed{} = 8^2$

$\boxed{} - 11 = 25$ $\qquad$ $6^2 + 13 = \boxed{}$

$7^2 - 6^2 = \boxed{}$ $\qquad$ $\boxed{}^2 - 8^2 = 17$

$64 - \boxed{} = 49$ $\qquad$ $3^2 - \boxed{}^2 = 5$

$>$, $=$, or $<$?

$4^2 \boxed{>} 2^2 + 2^2$ $\qquad\qquad$ $1^2 \times 1^2 \qquad 1^2$

$2^2 \qquad 2^2 \times 1^2$ $\qquad\qquad$ $0^2 \times 0^2 \qquad 0^2$

$3^2 + 4^2 \qquad 5^2$ $\qquad\qquad$ $10^2 - 8^2 \qquad 6^2$

$\qquad\qquad 2^2 \times 2^2 \qquad 4^2$

Ref: Lab Sheet Annotations, page 255.

•••••• P-17

Cross-Number Puzzle

across

A $880 \div 8$

C $5^2 + 2^2$

D 8×9

E 2^6

G $7 \times 9 \times 2 \times 5$

H $2^2 \times 2^2 \times 2^2 \times 2$

I $\frac{1}{3}$ of 57

J $5^2 \times 3$

K $\frac{1}{11}$ of 11^2

L 11^2

M $10^2 + 5^2 + 1^2$

down

A $\frac{1}{3}$ of 51

B $2^2 \times 3$

C $2 \times 10^2 + 2^2 \times 10$

E $\frac{1}{2} \times 1276$

F $10^3 - 1$

G $7^2 + 13$

H $4^2 - 1$

I $\frac{1}{9}$ of 999

J $7 \times 2 \times 5$

K $\frac{1}{4}$ of 48

L 24

Ref: *Lab Sheet Annotations*, page 255.

Name _____ Date _____

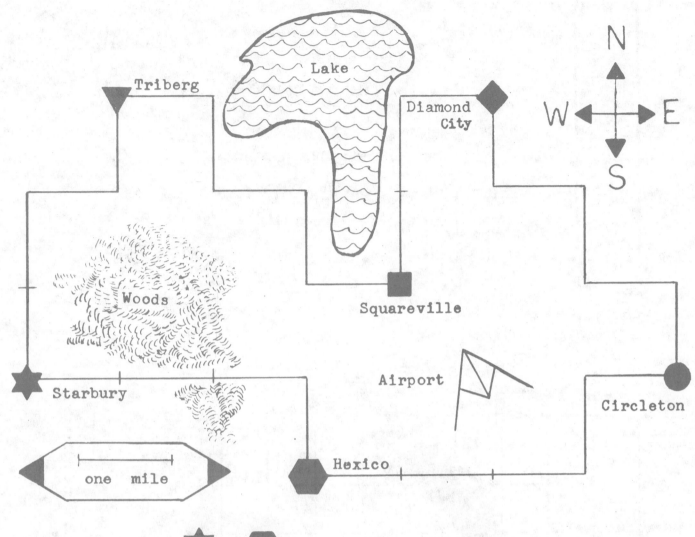

The road from ★ to ⬡ is _____ miles long.

It goes _____ miles East and _____ mile South.

The road from ⬡ to ● goes_____ miles East and_____ mile North.

The road from ● to ◆ goes_____ miles North and_____ miles West.

The road from ◆ to ■ goes_____ miles South and_____ miles West.

The road from ■ to ▼ goes 3 miles_____and 2 miles_____.

The road from ▼ to ★ goes 1 mile_____ and _____ miles_____.

An airplane flying from ★ **to** ● **would fly**_____ **miles East.**

An airplane flying from ● **to** ★ **would fly**_____ **miles**_____.

Ref: *Lab Sheet Annotations*, page 268.

●●●●●●●R-1

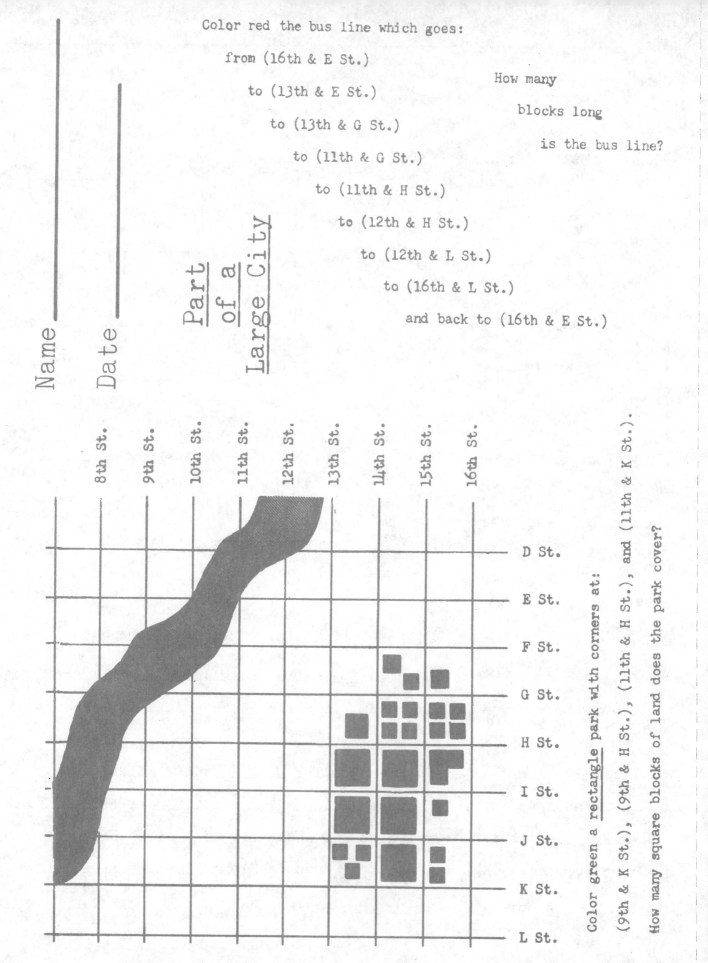

Color red the bus line which goes:

from (16th & E St.)

to (13th & E St.)

to (13th & G St.)

to (11th & G St.)

to (11th & H St.)

to (12th & H St.)

to (12th & L St.)

to (16th & L St.)

and back to (16th & E St.)

How many blocks long is the bus line?

Name

Date

Part of a Large City

Color green a rectangle park with corners at:

(9th & K St.), (9th & H St.), (11th & H St.), and (11th & K St.).

How many square blocks of land does the park cover?

Ref: *Lab Sheet Annotations*, page 268.

R-2

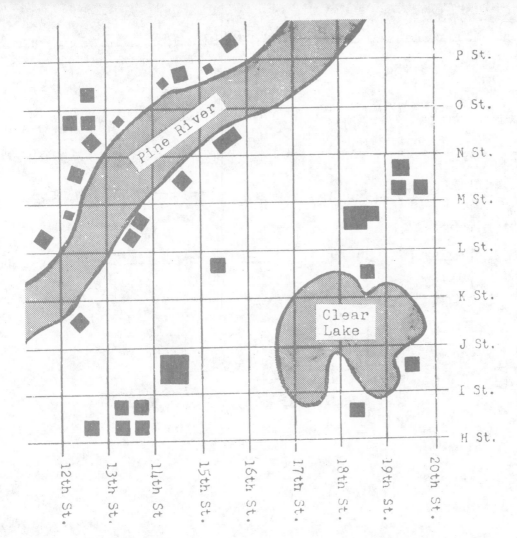

The new Pine River Expressway passes through these corners:

    (I St. & 12th),

    (J St. & 13th),

    (K St. & 14th),

    (L St. & 15th),

    (M St. & 16th),

    (N St. & 17th),

    (O St. & 18th), and

    (P St. & 19th).

A winding road goes around Clear Lake. It passes through these corners:

    (L St. & 18th),

    (J St. & 20th),

    (H St. & 18th), and

    (J St. & 16th).

Draw this road on the map.

Date

Name

Draw the expressway on the map.

A large bridge crosses the Pine River. It starts at (P St. & 13th) and goes to (M St. & 16th). Draw it on the map.

Ref: *Lab Sheet Annotations*, pages 268 and 269.

•••••• R-3

Name_____ Date_____

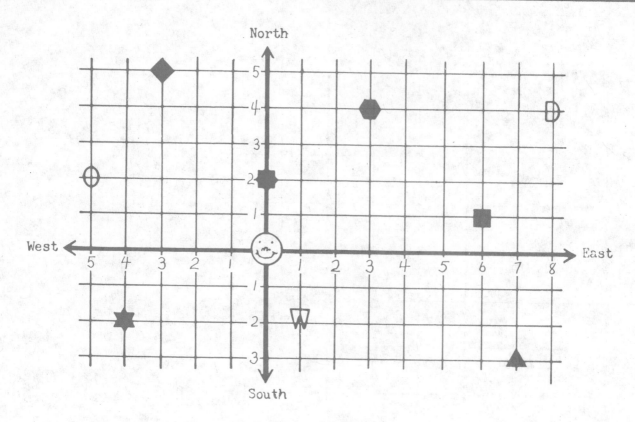

	East	West	North	South
⬡	3	—	4	—
◼		—		—
▲		—	—	
◆	—		—	
₩		—	—	

	E	W	N	S
○	—			—
★	—		—	
D		—		—
✹	0	0	2	—
☺				

Ref: *Lab Sheet Annotations*, page 269.

●●●●●●●R-4

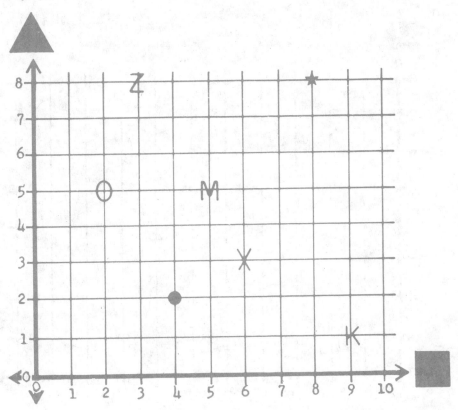

The ● is [4] over and [2] up.

The X is [ ] over and [ ] up.

The O is [ ] over and [ ] up.

The M is [ ] over and [ ] up.

The ★ is [ ] over and [ ] up.

The K is [ ] over and [ ] up.

The Z is [ ] over and [ ] up.

■	▲
4	2

Ref: *Lab Sheet Annotations*, page 270.

●●●●●●● R-5

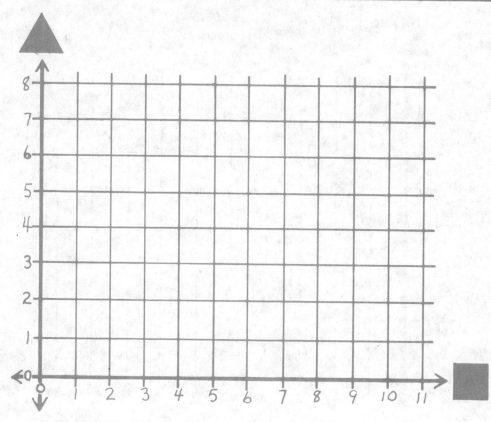

■	▲
Write X at	3	2
Write ● at	5	6
Write ◇ at	7	3
Write ⊗ at	4	4
Write B at	5	0
Write W at	1	7
Write H at	0	3

Ref: *Lab Sheet Annotations*, page 270.

Finish the patterns on the grids below.

Draw a straight line through all the points

on each of the grids.

The ◯ Pattern

The ✕ Pattern

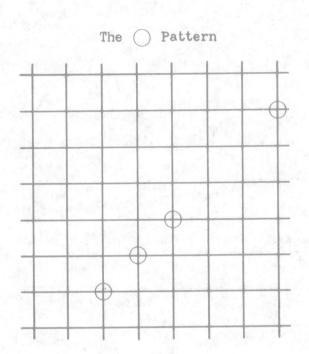

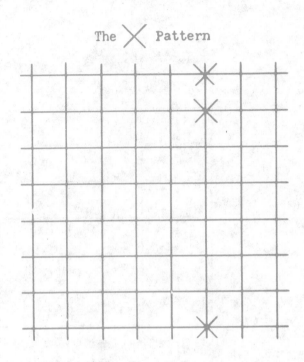

This is the ● Pattern.

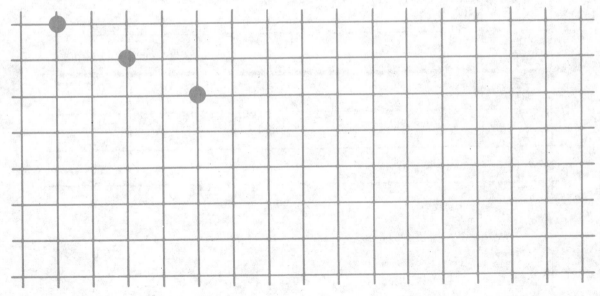

Ref: *Lab Sheet Annotations*, page 271.

On this grid are several straight line patterns.

Find each one and finish it. Add one of your own.

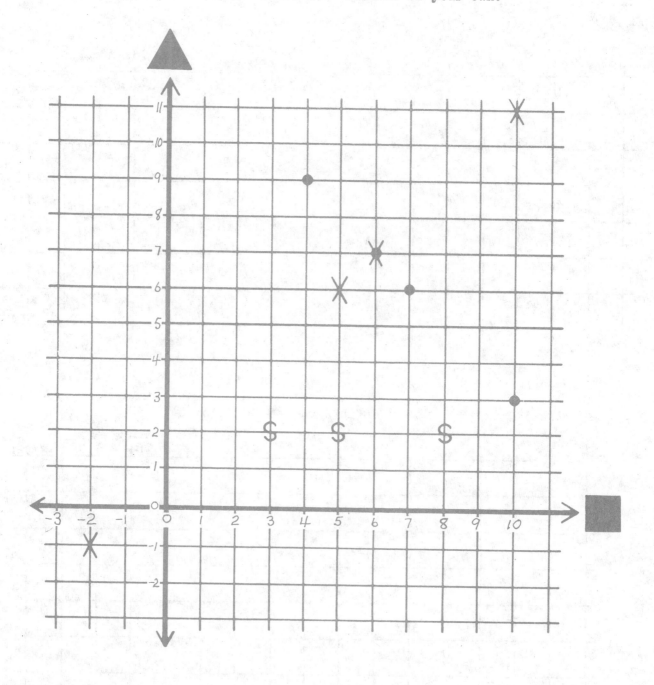

Ref: *Lab Sheet Annotations*, page 271.   ●●●●●●●R-8

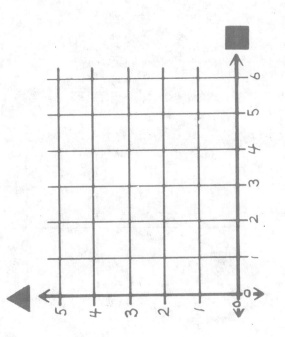

Make dots at these points:

▲	■
5	5
4	4
3	3
2	2
1	1
0	0

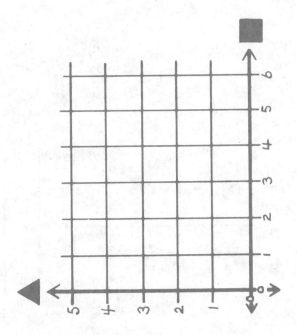

Make dots at these points:

▲	■
1	4
2	3
3	2
4	1
5	0
0	5

Now draw a line that passes through all the dots.

Name

Date

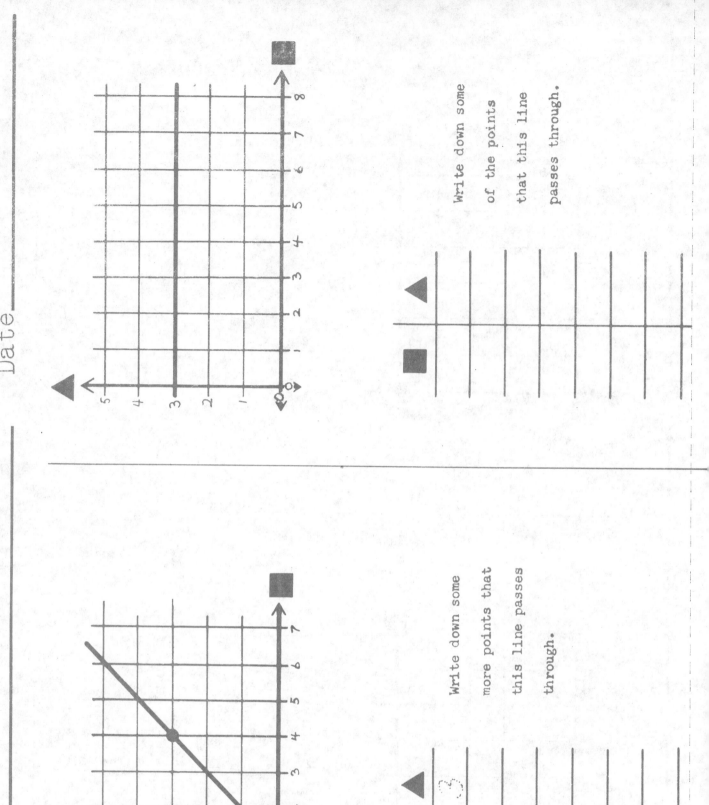

Write down some
of the points
that this line
passes through.

Write down some
more points that
this line passes
through.

Ref: *Lab Sheet Annotations*, page 272.

Name _____

Date _____

In how many different ways can you make these open
sentences true?

$\blacksquare + \blacktriangle = 9$

$\blacksquare - \blacktriangle = 2$

$\blacksquare + 4 = \blacktriangle$

$0 + 4 = 4$

$1 + 4 = 5$

$2 + 4 = 6$

$3 + 4 = \triangle$

$\square + 4 = \triangle$

$\square + 4 = \triangle$

$\square + 4 = $

$\square + 4 = $

$+ 4 = $

$+ 4 = $

Ref: *Lab Sheet Annotations*, page 273.

Name _____

Date _____

Make these open sentences true in as many different ways as you can. Then fill in the charts with the ■ and ▲ numbers.

■ + 7 = ▲
2 + 7 = 9
5 + 7 = 12
6 + 7 = △
□ + 7 = △

■	▲
2	9
5	12
6	△
□	△
□	△
□	△

■ + ▲ = 6

▲
■

Ref: *Lab Sheet Annotations*, page 273.

•••••••R-12

Name _____

Date _____

This page is about the open sentence ■ + 3 = ▲

Finish the chart, and then find the points on the graph.

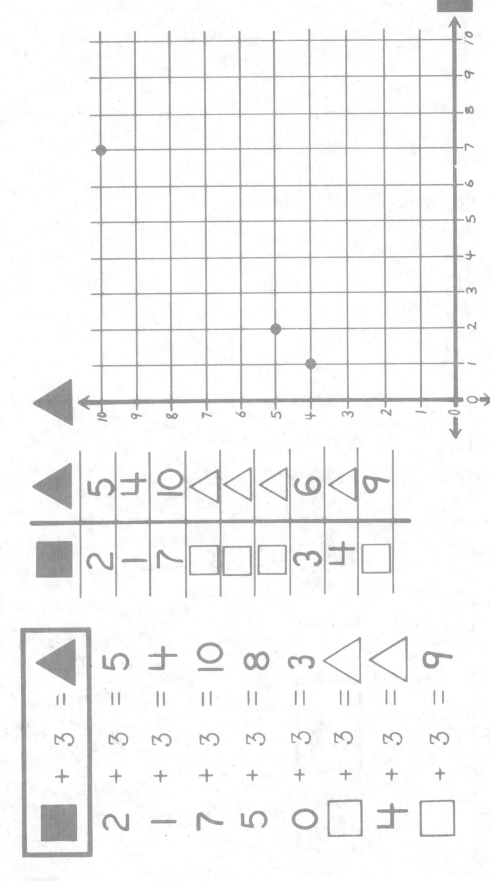

■ + 3 = ▲
2 + 3 = 5
1 + 3 = 4
7 + 3 = 10
5 + 3 = 8
0 + 3 = 3
□ + 3 = ◁
4 + 3 = ◁
□ + 3 = 9

▲	■
5	2
4	1
10	7
◁	□
◁	□
◁	□
6	3
◁	4
9	□

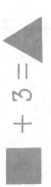

Draw a straight line which goes through all of the points which you have plotted.

Ref: *Lab Sheet Annotations*, page 274.

Name _____

Date _____

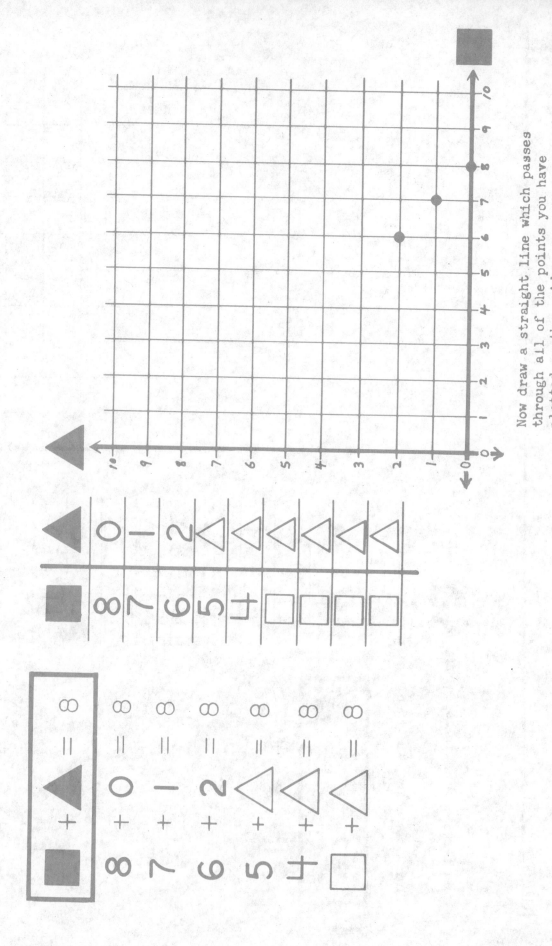

Now draw a straight line which passes through all of the points you have plotted on the grid.

Ref: *Lab Sheet Annotations*, page 274.

●●●●●● R-14

Name _____

Date _____

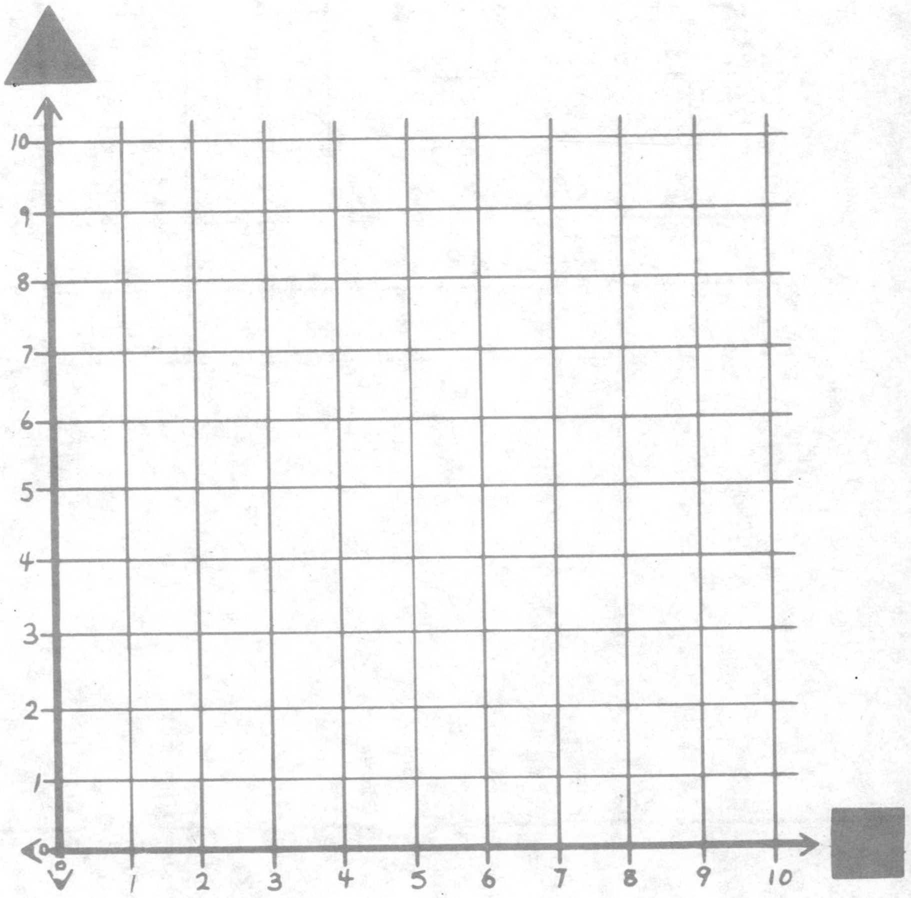

◀ 5 = 1 + 4

8 = 1 + 7

10 = 1 + 9

Ref: *Lab Sheet Annotations*, page 275.

••••••• R-15

■ = 10 - ▲

6 = 10 - 4

5 = 10 - 5

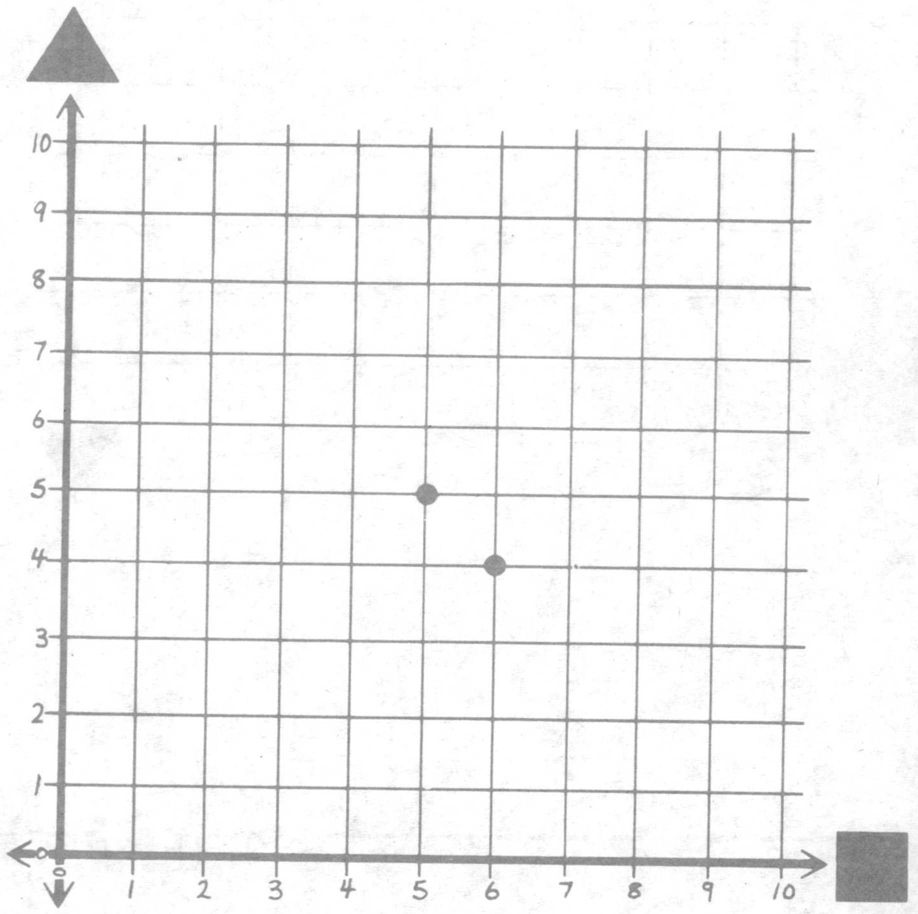

10 = 10 - ◁

□ = 10 - ◁

□ = 10 - ◁

Ref: *Lab Sheet Annotations*, page 275.

Name _____

Date _____

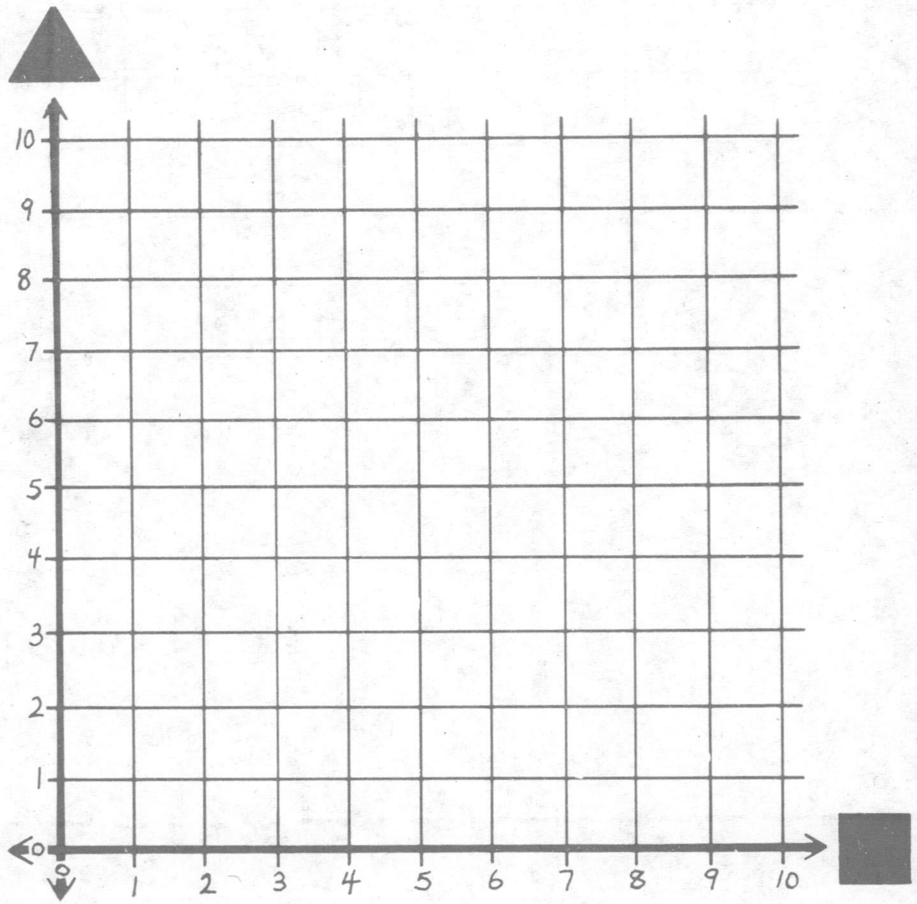

▣ ◀ = ◀ - 2

4 = 6 - 2

7 = 9 - 2

Ref: *Lab Sheet Annotations*, page 275.

•••••• R-17

Name _____

Date _____

Beware: This problem is tricky.

$$\boxed{\blacksquare + \blacktriangle = \blacktriangle + 3}$$

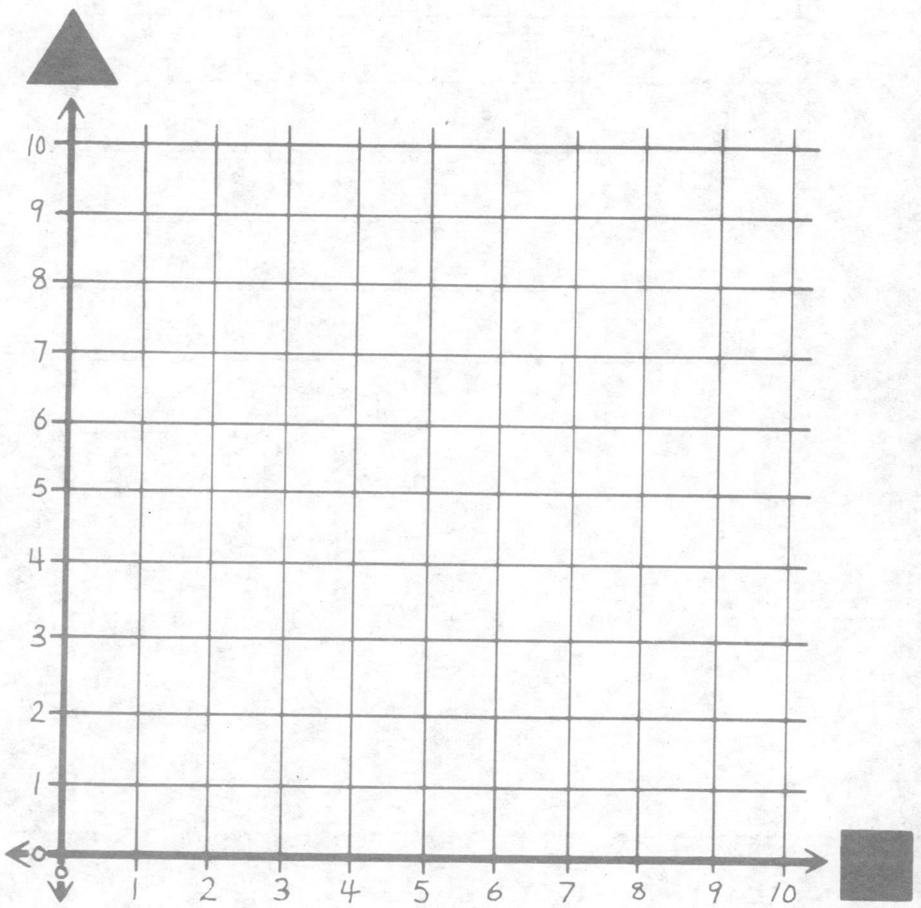

Ref: *Lab Sheet Annotations*, page 276.

	⬛	🔺
Write ◆ at	5	3
Write ○ at	5	-2
Write ✕ at	2	6
Write ● at	-4	6
Write ⧉ at	-4	3
Write ⊠ at	-4	-2
Write Z at	-2	4

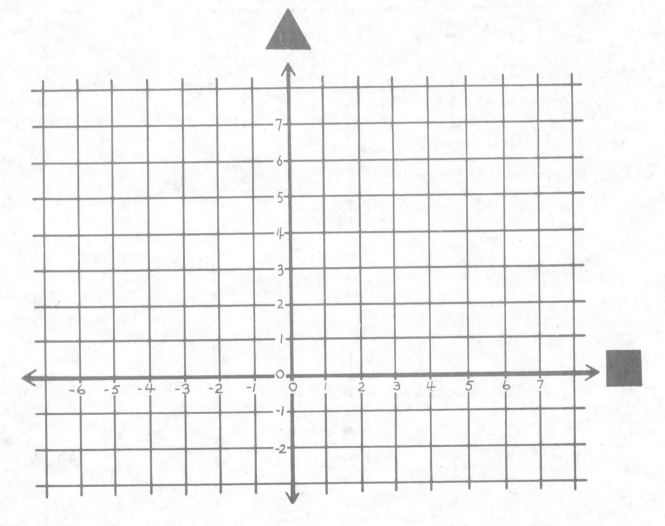

Ref: *Lab Sheet Annotations*, page 276.

• • • • • • • R-19

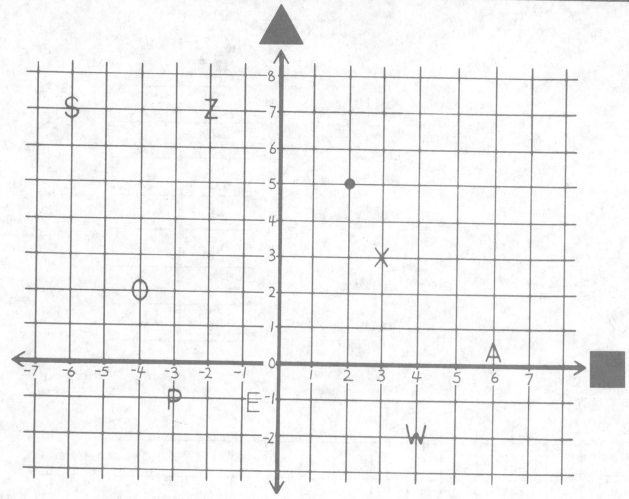

Finish this

chart by

looking at

the graph.

	■	▲
O →	4	2
X →		
Z →		
W →		
P →		
• →		
A →		
S →		
E →		

Ref: *Lab Sheet Annotations*, page 276.

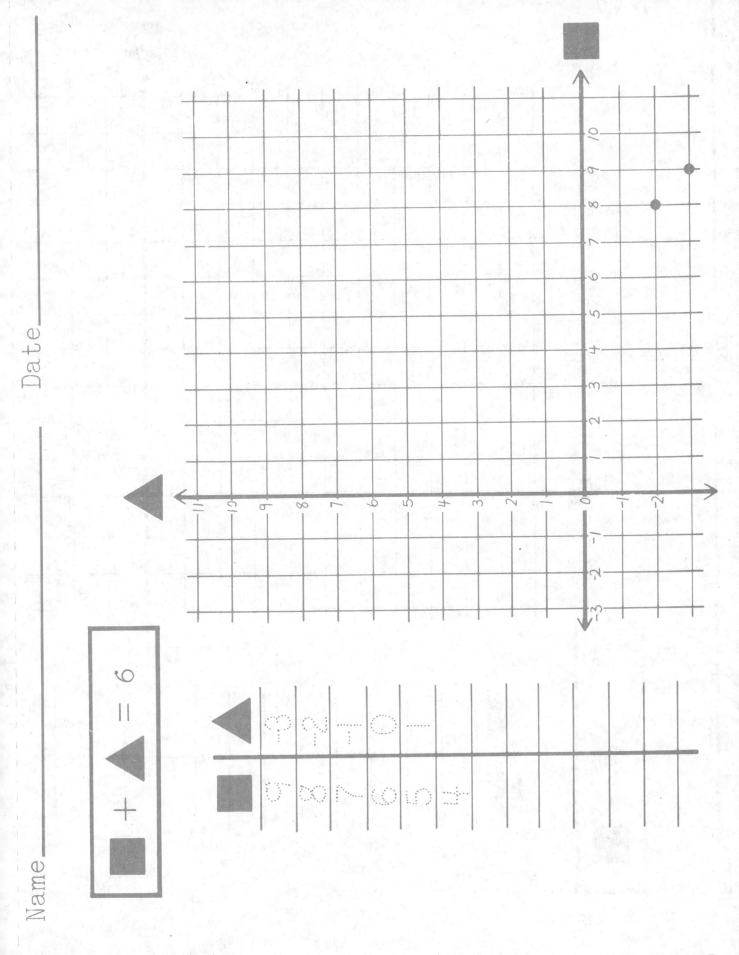

■ + ▲ = 6

Ref: *Lab Sheet Annotations*, page 277.

Name

Date

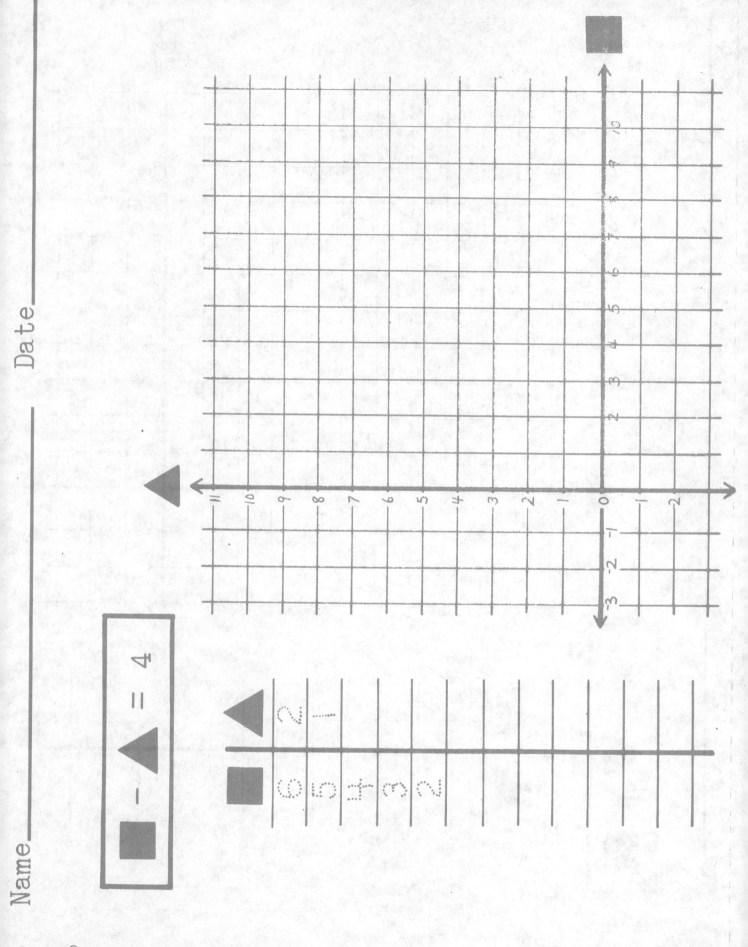

Ref: *Lab Sheet Annotations*, page 278.

•••••••R-22

Name

Date

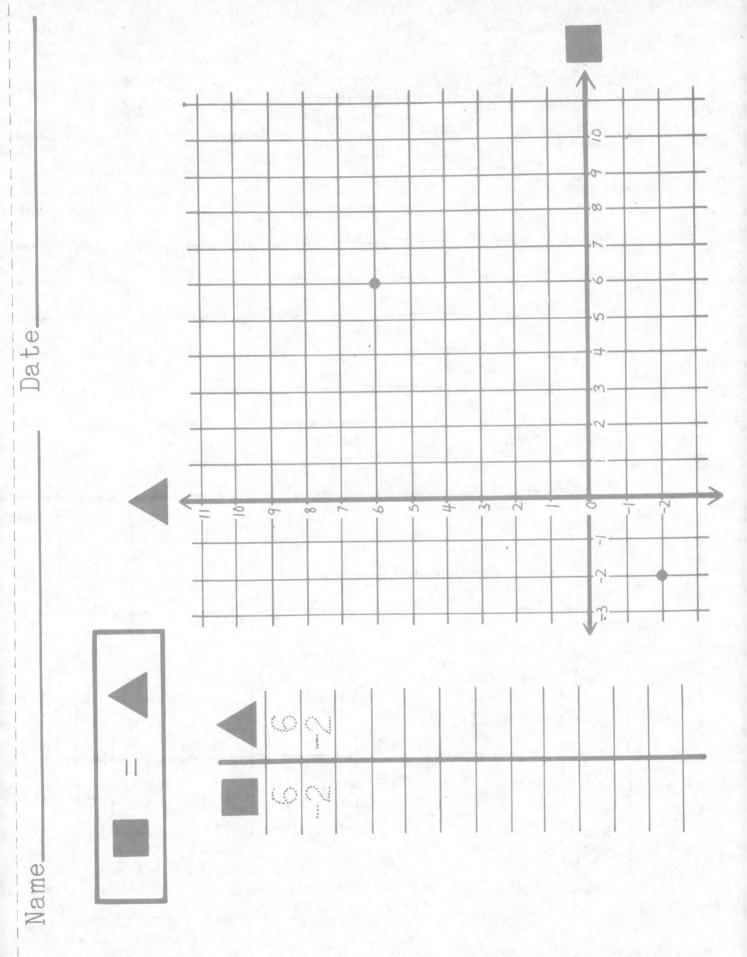

Ref: *Lab Sheet Annotations*, page 278.

•••••••R-23

Name _____

Date _____

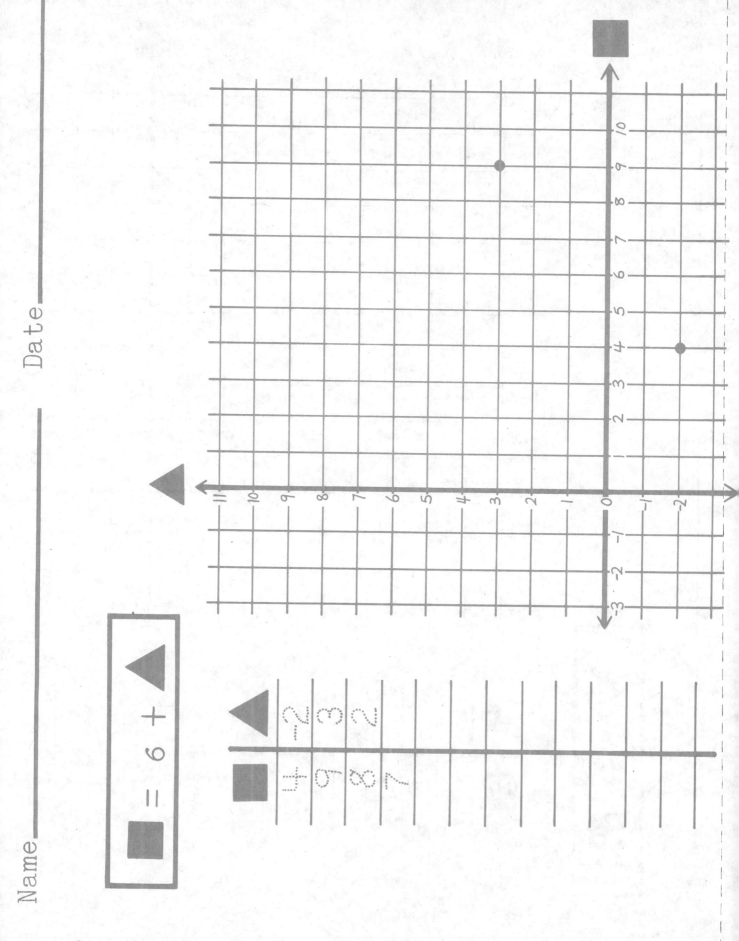

Ref: *Lab Sheet Annotations*, page 279.

●●●●●●R-24

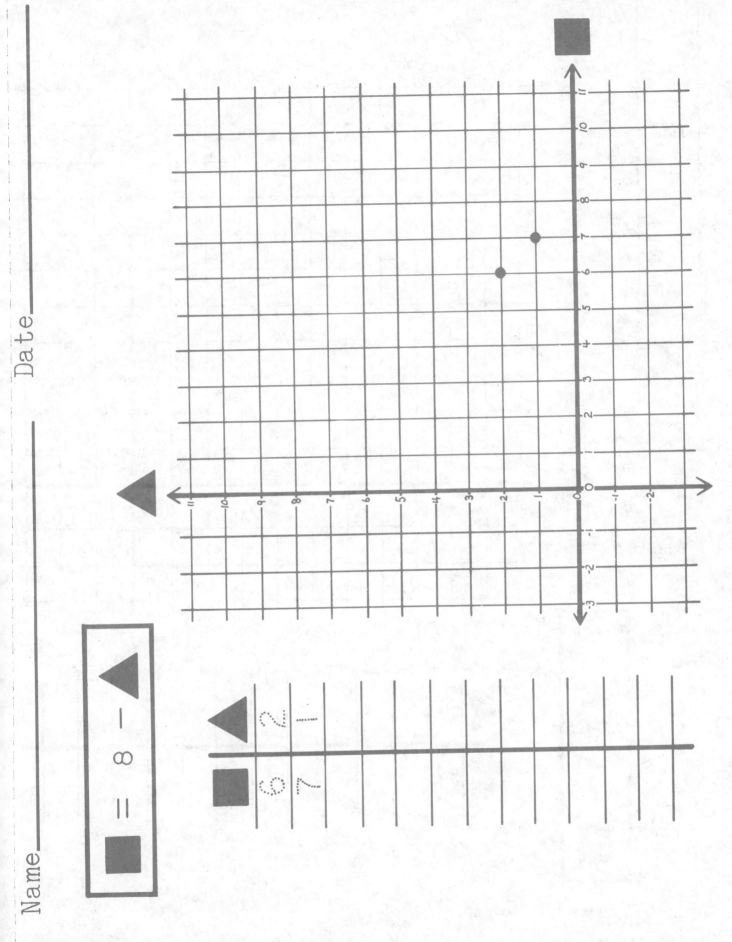

Name _____

Date _____

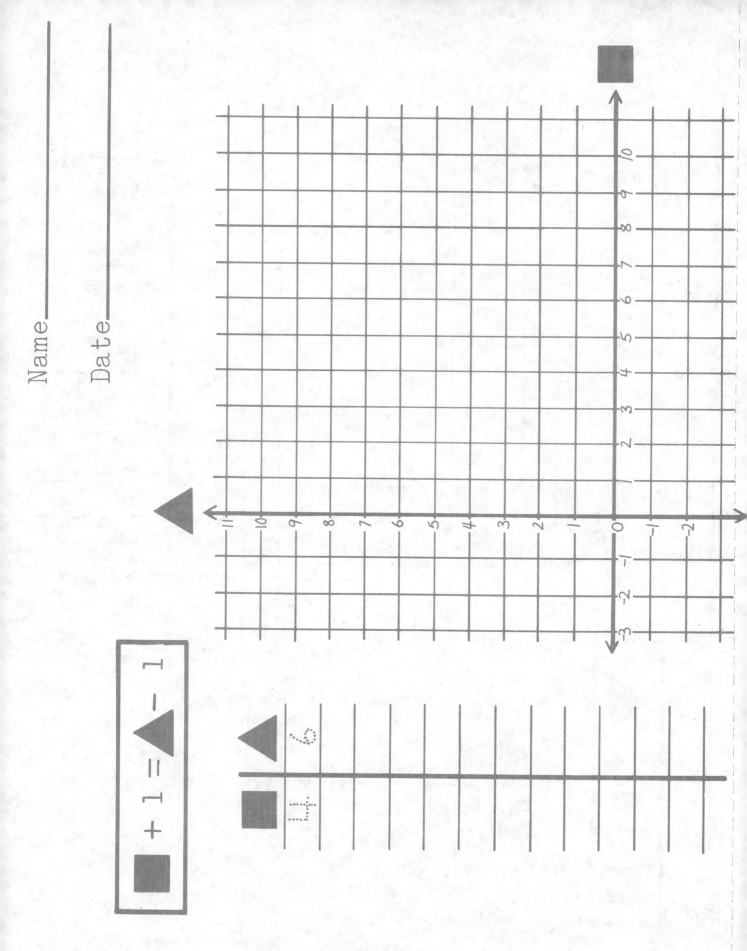

Ref: *Lab Sheet Annotations*, page 280.

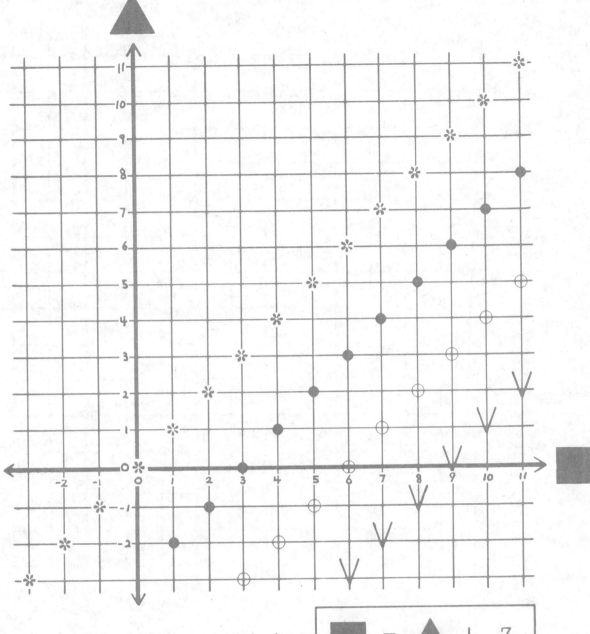

A rule for the ● points is: ■ = ▲ + 3 •

See if you can find the rules for the other sets of points.

The ○ rule is:  •

The V rule is: 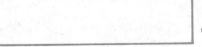 •

The ✳ rule is:  •

Ref: *Lab Sheet Annotations*, page 280.

●●●●●●●R-27

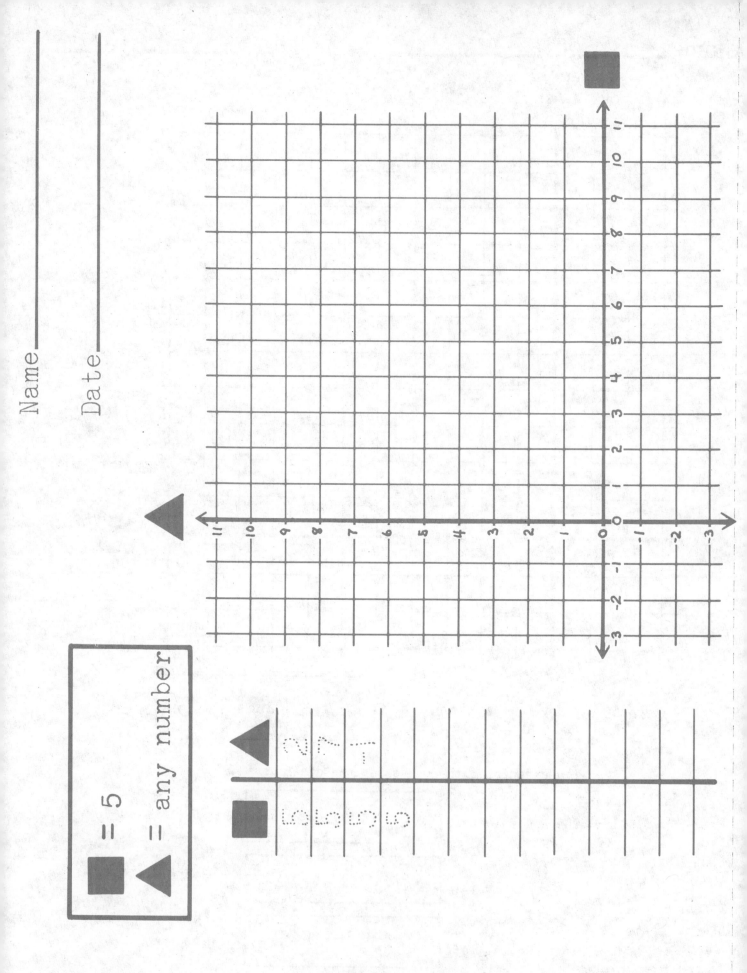

Name

Date

■ = 5

◀ = any number

Ref: *Lab Sheet Annotations*, page 281.

Make up your own rule to graph.

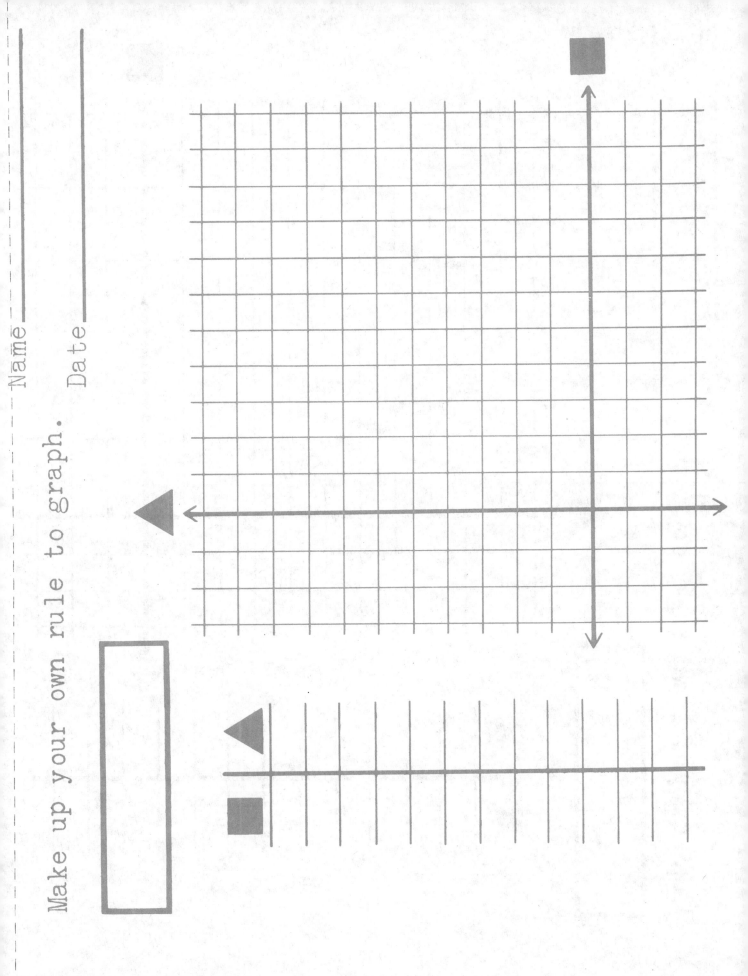

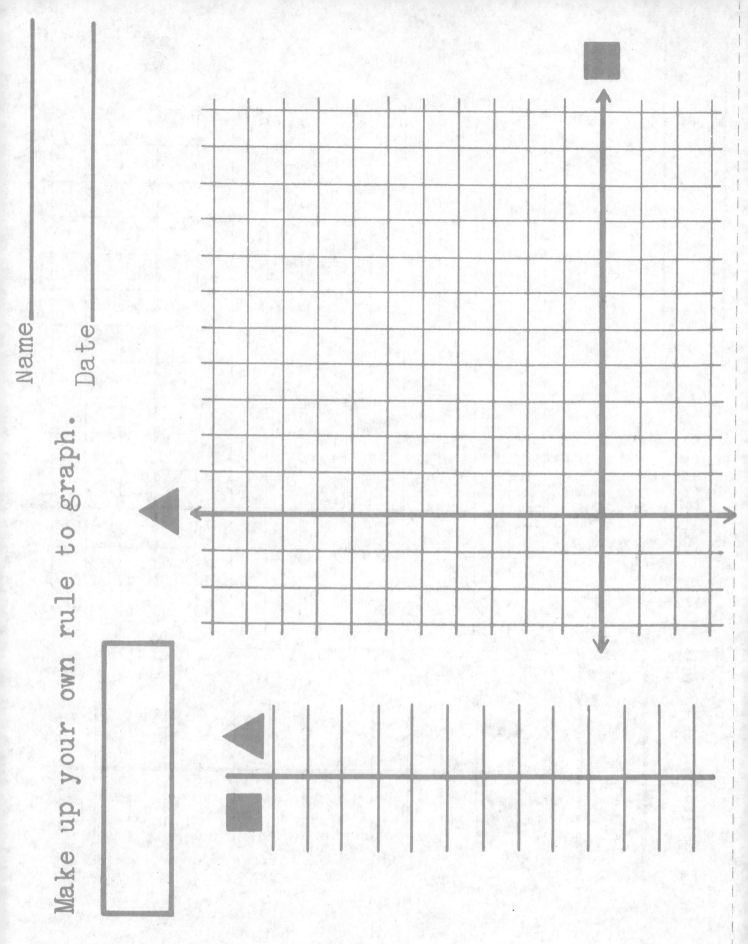

Name

Date

Make up your own rule to graph.

Name_____ Date_____

Arrow Problems

Finish this chart. Then use it to
solve the arrow problems below.

1	3	6	10	15				
2	5	9	14	20				
4	8	13	19	26				
7	12	18	25	33				
11	17	24	32	41				

****-means
extra tricky**

1 → → = ⬡

5 ↓ = ⬡

7 → → ↑ = ⬡

25 ↓ ← ← = ⬡   32 ↓ → → ↑↑ = ⬡

11 ↓ = ⬡   9 ↓↓↓↓ = ⬡

20 ↑ → = ⬡   1 → → → → → → → = ⬡

33 → = ⬡   1 → → → → → → ↓ = ⬡

41 ↓ → = ⬡   **34 ↓↓ = ⬡

Ref: *Lab Sheet Annotations*, page 320.

Name _____

Date _____

Finish filling in this grid.

Then solve these arrow problems.

3	0	1	2	3	
0		2	3	0	1
1	2	3	0		2
2	3			2	3
3	0	1	2	3	0
	1	2		0	1
		3	0		
			1		3

1 → ⬡

2 → ⬡

3 → ⬡

0 → ⬡

2 → → → → ⬡

3 → → → → ⬡

1 ↓↓↓↓ ⬡

⬡ ↓↓↓↓ 3

⬡ ↑↑↑↑ 0

2 → ↓ → ↓ ⬡

1 → ↓↓↓ ⬡

2 → ↑ ⬡

0 → ↑ → ↑ → ↑ → ⬡

1 ← ↓ ← ↓ ⬡

3 ← → ← ↓↓↓ ⬡

0 ↑↑↑↑ → → → → ⬡

2 ↑ ← ⬡

2 ↑↑ ← ← ⬡

2 ↑↑↑ ← ← ← ⬡

Ref: *Lab Sheet Annotations*, page 322.

●●●●●●● V-10

Name _____ Date _____

THE CLOCK IS

MAGIC!

It runs backward ↻

and runs forward ↺

$3 \circlearrowright 2 = 5$

BUT $3 \circlearrowleft 2 = 1$

Magic Clock Problems:

$6 \circlearrowleft 4 = \square$
$6 \circlearrowright 4 = \square$
$9 \circlearrowright 4 = \square$
$9 \circlearrowleft 4 = \square$

$4 \circlearrowright 12 = \square$
$4 \circlearrowleft 12 = \square$

$11 \circlearrowleft 6 = \square$
$11 \circlearrowright 6 = \square$
$3 \circlearrowright 6 = \square$
$3 \circlearrowleft 6 = \square$

$5 \circlearrowright 11 = \square$
$5 \circlearrowleft 11 = \square$

Make up your own problems:

forward

↺ =

↺ =

backward

↻ =

↻ =

Ref: *Lab Sheet Annotations*, page 339.

•••••• X-17

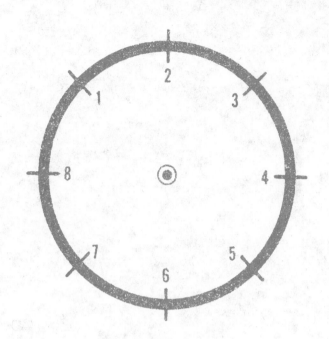

MAGIC

CLOCK

4 ⟳ 2 = ☐   1 ⟳ 3 = ☐
4 ⟲ 2 = ☐   1 ⟳ 3 = ☐

3 ⟲ 8 = ☐   6 ⟳ 4 = ☐
3 ⟳ 8 = ☐   6 ⟲ 4 = ☐

7 ⟲ 8 = ☐   8 ⟳ 4 = ☐
7 ⟳ 8 = ☐   8 ⟲ 4 = ☐

2 ⟳ 16 = ☐   5 ⟳ 12 = ☐
2 ⟲ 16 = ☐   5 ⟲ 12 = ☐

3 ⟳ 2 = ☐   7 ⟲ 3 = ☐
3 ⟳ 10 = ☐   7 ⟲ 11 = ☐

Ref: *Lab Sheet Annotations*, page 339.

Name _____

Date _____

Guessing Games

about Sets of Things

Look at this picture.

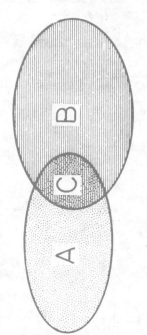

In set A are books.

In set B are red things.

In set C are _____

Look at this picture:

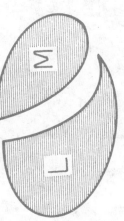
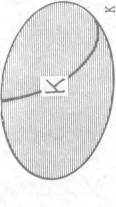

L is the set of boys.

M is the set of girls.

K is the set of _____

Look at this picture:

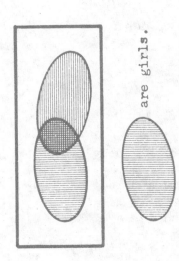

_____ are girls.

_____ are babies.

_____ are _____

Ref: *Lab Sheet Annotations*, page 345.

●●●●●●●Y-1

Name_____   Date_____

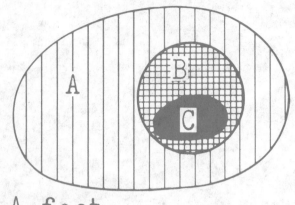

This picture is about three things:

parts of the body,

parts of the face, and

parts of the eye.

A foot

Is a foot a part of the body?   YES   NO

Is a foot a part of the face?   YES   NO

Is a foot a part of the eye?   YES   NO

Therefore a foot belongs in - - - - - SET A   SET B   SET C

A mouth

Is a mouth a part of the body?   YES   NO

Is a mouth a part of the face?   YES   NO

Is a mouth a part of the eye?   YES   NO

Therefore a mouth belongs in - - - - -SET A   SET B   SET C

An eyelid

Is an eyelid a part of the body?   YES   NO

Is an eyelid a part of the face?   YES   NO

Is an eyelid a part of the eye?   YES   NO

Therefore an eyelid belongs in - - - - SET A   SET B   SET C

Ref: *Lab Sheet Annotations*, page 346.   ●●●●●●●●Y-2

Name_____ Date_____

Look at this picture:

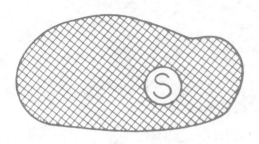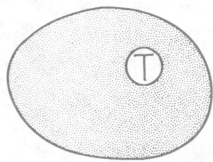

None of set S is in set T, and none of set T is in set S.

S could be the set of dogs,

and T could be the set of cats,

since no dogs are cats,

and no cats are dogs.

_____

Or S could be the set of [   ],

and T could be the set of (_____),

since no [   ] are (_____),

and no (_____) are [   ].

_____

Or S could be the set of [   ],

and T could be the set of (_____),

since no [   ] are (_____),

and no (_____) are [   ].

Ref: *Lab Sheet Annotations*, page 346.   ●●●●●●●Y-3

Look at this picture:

All of set P is in set Q, and some of set Q is in set P.

P could be the set of ROSES.

and Q could be the set of FLOWERS,

since all ROSES are FLOWERS,

and some FLOWERS are ROSES.

OR P could be the set of [   ]

and Q could be the set of (   )

since all [   ] are (   )

and some (   ) are [   ]

OR P could be the set of [   ]

and Q could be the set of (   )

since all [   ] are (   )

and some (   ) are [   ]

Ref: *Lab Sheet Annotations*, page 347.

Look at this picture:

Some of set X is in set Z, and some of set Z is in set X.

X could be the set of TEACHERS,

and Z could be the set of MEN,

since some TEACHERS are MEN,

and some MEN are TEACHERS.

OR X could be the set of [   ]

and Z could be the set of (   )

since some [   ] are (   )

and some (   ) are [   ]

OR X could be the set of [   ]

and Z could be the set of (   )

since some [   ] are (   )

and some (   ) are [   ]

Ref: *Lab Sheet Annotations*, page 347.

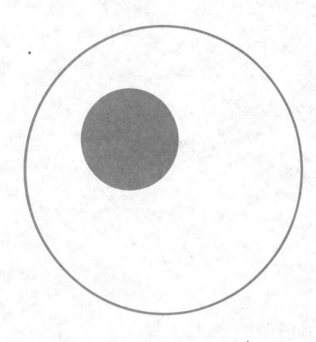
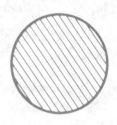

This diagram shows three sets of things:

       the set of all four legged animals,

       the set of all ducks, and

       the set of all dogs.

The striped circle shows the set of _____.

The white circle shows the set of _____.

The dark circle shows the set of _____.

Put a cross in the diagram where a cat would belong.

Draw a circle to show the set of fish. Shade it with dots.

Draw a circle to show the set of all animals that have
wings and feathers. (Remember that ducks have wings and
feathers.) Color this circle yellow.

Ref: *Lab Sheet Annotations*, page 348.

●●●●●●●Y-6

Name _____ Date _____

Which Diagram Fits Best?

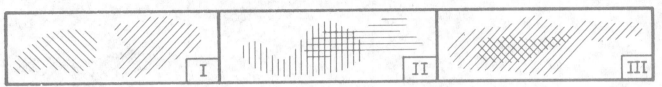

| I | II | III |

No
Some
All   OAK TREES are PLANTS.

No
Some
All   PLANTS are OAK TREES.

Which diagram tells that story?   I   II   III

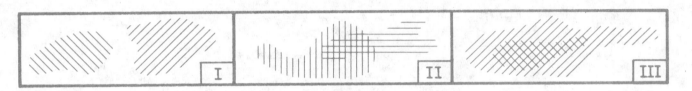

No
Some
All   GIRLS are PEOPLE WHO

WEAR GLASSES.

No
Some
All   PEOPLE WHO WEAR GLASSES

are GIRLS.

Which diagram tells that story?   I   II   III

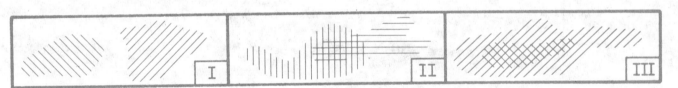

No
Some
All   ANIMALS WITH FUR are

TELEPHONES.

No
Some
All   TELEPHONES are ANIMALS

WITH FUR.

Which diagram tells that story?   I   II   III

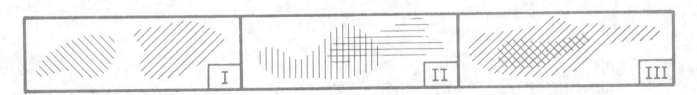

No
Some
All   ODD NUMBERS are EVEN

NUMBERS.

No
Some
All   EVEN NUMBERS are ODD

NUMBERS.

Which diagram tells that story?   I   II   III

Ref: *Lab Sheet Annotations*, page 349.

Name _____ Date _____

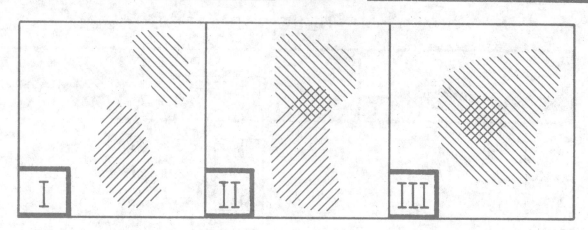

No
Some
All

NUMBERS BETWEEN 0 AND 1 are NUMBERS GREATER THAN 10.

Which diagram fits best?   I   II   III

No
Some
All

NUMBERS GREATER THAN 10 are NUMBERS BETWEEN 0 AND 1.

No
Some
All

SQUARE NUMBERS are EVEN NUMBERS.

Which diagram fits best?   I   II   III

No
Some
All

EVEN NUMBERS are SQUARE NUMBERS.

No
Some
All

FACTORS OF 6 are FACTORS OF 12.

Which diagram fits best?   I   II   III

No
Some
All

FACTORS OF 12 are FACTORS OF 6.

No
Some
All

FACTORS OF 9 are FACTORS OF 6.

Which diagram fits best?   I   II   III

No
Some
All

FACTORS OF 6 are FACTORS OF 9.

Ref: *Lab Sheet Annotations*, page 349.

●●●●●●● Y-8

Name_____ Date_____

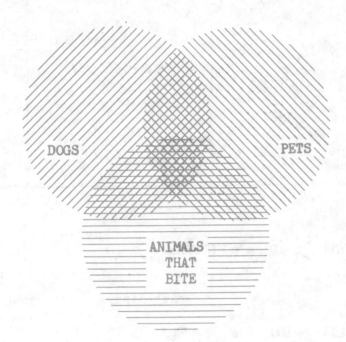

| stands for the set of all DOGS. | stands for the set of all PETS. | stands for the set of all ANIMALS THAT BITE. |

 stands for the set of _____

 stands for the set of _____

 stands for the set of _____

stands for the set of _____

Ref: *Lab Sheet Annotations*, page 350.

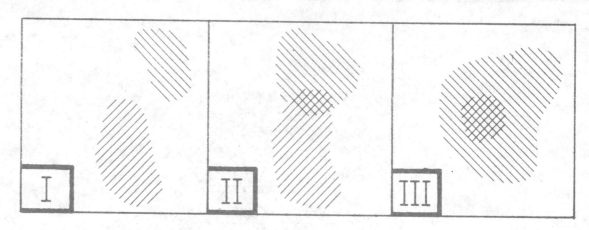

No Some **All**	NUMBERS > 10 are NUMBERS > 100.
	Which diagram fits best? I II· III
No Some **All**	NUMBERS > 100 are NUMBERS > 10.
No Some **All**	NUMBERS < 20 are NUMBERS > 20.
	Which diagram fits best? I II III
No Some **All**	NUMBERS > 20 are NUMBERS < 20.

No Some **All**	ODD NUMBERS are FACTORS OF 5.
	Which diagram fits best? I II III
No Some **All**	FACTORS OF 5 are ODD NUMBERS.
No Some **All**	PRIME NUMBERS are ODD NUMBERS.
	Which diagram fits best? I II III
No Some **All**	ODD NUMBERS are PRIME NUMBERS.

Ref: *Lab Sheet Annotations*, pages 349 and 351.   ●●●●●● Y-10

I had one dollar.

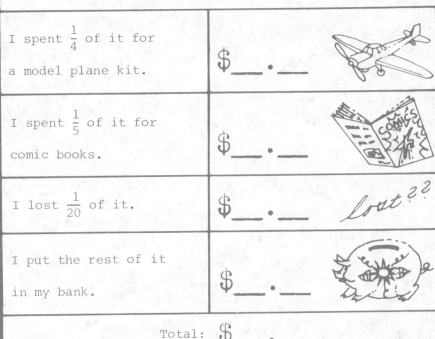

Name: _____

I spent $\frac{1}{4}$ of it for a model plane kit.	$ ___ . ___
I spent $\frac{1}{5}$ of it for comic books.	$ ___ . ___
I lost $\frac{1}{20}$ of it.	$ ___ . ___
I put the rest of it in my bank.	$ ___ . ___

Date: _____

Total: $ ___ . ___

Ms. Fixit gave Bert 16 square tiles, each 10 centimeters long. He laid

them on the square-shaped floor of his doll house. They fit exactly.

How long is Bert's floor? [____] cm, or ⬡ m long.

How wide is it? [____] cm, or ⬡ m long.

Mother's Purse

Mother said, "Boys, each of you can have

$\frac{1}{3}$ of the money in my purse. There is

less than 40 cents in my purse.

   Three coins are for Bill.

   Two coins are for Ben.

   Eleven coins are for Paul."

How much money did each boy get? ⟶ [____]

How much money was in the purse? △

When you are finished with this page, turn it over and write a word
problem of your own.

Ref: *Lab Sheet Annotations*, page 356.

•••••• Z-1

Name _____ Date_____

At the left of the pictures are abbreviations for many units of measure, such as second (sec.) and dollar ($). Each measure goes with a picture. Find where it goes and write the abbreviation.

sec.

pt.

l

gal.

min.

¢

cm²

c.

$

qt.

°C
degrees Celsius

hr.

20 _____

12 _____ on a clock

60 _____ in an hour

60 _____ in a minute

_____ 1.00

a 22 _____ stamp

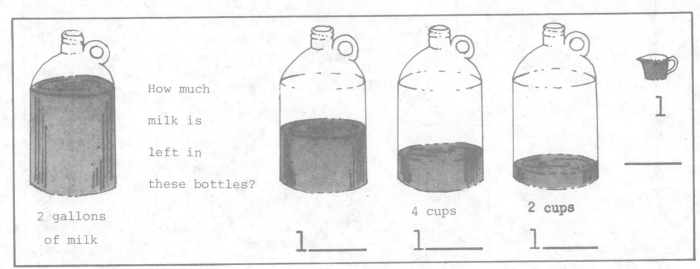

How much milk is left in these bottles?

2 gallons of milk

1 _____   4 cups   2 cups   1

1 _____   1 _____   1 _____

Ref: *Lab Sheet Annotations*, page 356.

•••••••Z-2

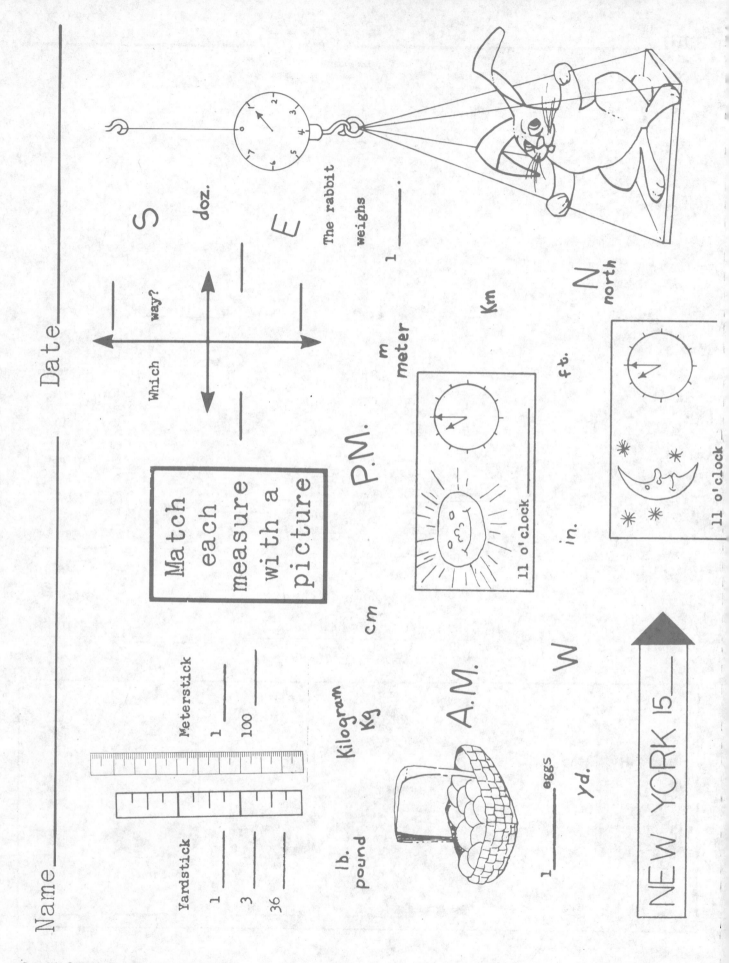

Name

Date

Match each measure with a picture

Meterstick
1 ____
100 ____

Yardstick
1 ____
3 ____
36 ____

Kilogram
Kg ____

lb.
pound ____

cm ____

A.M.

P.M.

W

N
north

S

E

doz. ____

The rabbit
weighs
1 ____ .

Which ____ way?

m
meter ____

Km ____

ft. ____

in. ____

eggs
1 ____

yd. ____

11 o'clock ____

11 o'clock ____

NEW YORK 15 ____

Ref: *Lab Sheet Annotations,* pages 356 and 357.

Name _____ Date _____

Can you solve these puzzles?

<u>pennies</u> only   <u>dimes</u> only   <u>dollars</u> only

Jim's money

Bob's money

Carol's money

59 coins   11 coins   1 coin

Who has the most money?   Jim   Bob   Carol

Who has the most coins?   Jim   Bob   Carol

4 of Bob's coins are worth as much as ☐ of Jim's coins.

Jim needs ☐ more coins to have as much money as Bob.

_____

Pam is 120 cm tall now.

At birth she was $\frac{4}{10}$ as tall.

How tall was Pam at birth? ☐ cm

Ref: *Lab Sheet Annotations*, page 357.

 Z-4

Which is box A, box B, box C, box D?

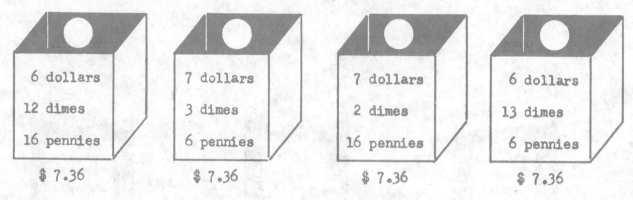

6 dollars	7 dollars	7 dollars	6 dollars
12 dimes	3 dimes	2 dimes	13 dimes
16 pennies	6 pennies	16 pennies	6 pennies
$ 7.36	$ 7.36	$ 7.36	$ 7.36

Each of the four boxes contains $7.36.

Each box has a different number of silver dollars, dimes, and pennies.

Read the three sentences below.

They will help you find out which

is box A, box B, box C, and box D.

Write the correct letter in the circle on each box.

Then check your answers by reading the sentences again.

$ 1.18 - I <u>cannot</u> take it out of A or B.

$ 5.43 - I <u>cannot</u> take it out of A or C.

$ 4.57 - I <u>can</u> take it out of <u>D only</u>.

Ref: *Lab Sheet Annotations*, page 358. •••••••Z-5

Name_____ Date_____

- - - - - - fold here - - - - - - - - - - -

Ref: *Lab Sheet Annotations*, page 358.

•••••••Z-6

①

Read this book about Simon and Sue.

Answer all the questions.

Then write another Simon and Sue story problem here.

⑥

Simon says, "Sue, you <u>wasted questions</u>.

You asked 9 questions to find my number.

I can <u>always</u> guess a whole number between

0 and 100 in <u>only 7 questions</u>."

<u>Which is Sue's most wasteful question?</u>

<u>Cross it out.</u>

You play the game with somebody in your class. Try to guess the number in only 7 questions.

Ref: *Lab Sheet Annotations*, page 358.

●●●●●●●Z-7

Baseball Cards

Simon and Sue are twins. They both

collect baseball cards. Simon has 143 cards.

Sue has 95 cards. Simon has 12 cards that

are the same as 12 of Sue's cards.

How many cards do they have together?

□ baseball cards

How many <u>different</u> cards do they have?

△ different cards

Name: _____

Date: _____

-------------------------------fold here-------------------------------

The Guessing Game

Simon plays a guessing game with Sue.

Simon: "I am thinking of a whole number

between 0 and 100. I will count

the number of questions you ask

to guess my number."

Simon:

"No."

"No."

"No."

"Yes."

"No."

"No."

"Yes."

"No."

"Yes!"

Sue:

"Is it between 80 and 100?"

"Is it between 50 and 80?"

"Is it between 60 and 30?"

"Is it an even number?"

"Does it end with a 5?"

"Does it end with a 2?"

"Does it end with a 4 or a 6?"

"Is it less than 20?"

"Then the NUMBER is _____."

⑤

Ref: *Lab Sheet Annotations*, page 358.

How Tall?

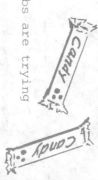

Simon is $\frac{1}{10}$ of a meter taller than Sue.

Sue has grown 5 centimeters since last
fall when she was 120 cm tall.

How tall is Sue now? ☐ cm

How tall is Simon? ☐ cm

C-A-N-D-Y

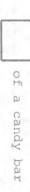

Simon, Sue, Buster and Barbs are trying

to divide evenly three candy bars.

How much should each child get?

☐ of a candy bar

The Present

Simon, Sue, and Sara buy a present

for a sick friend. Each brings half

a dollar to the store. The present

costs $1.26.

How much change does each child get?

$ ☐ . ☐ ☐ change for each child

When Was Barbs Born?

Simon and Sue were born on Feb. 1st in

a leap year. Barbs is 370 days younger

than Simon and Sue.

Barbs was born on

_____
(month, day)

of the next year.

Ref: *Lab Sheet Annotations*, page 358.

Name_____   Date_____

Bill gets $\frac{4}{5}$ as many

as Bob and Bruce

together get.

Bruce gets 30 marbles.

Bob gets $\frac{2}{3}$ as many as Bruce gets.

How many marbles are Bob's share? ☐ marbles

How many marbles go to Bill? ⬡ marbles

How many marbles are in the bag? △ marbles

How many marbles would each boy get if the marbles were

divided evenly? ◯ marbles

Martha gets 18 charms.

Mary gets $\frac{6}{5}$ as

many as Mimi.

Mimi gets $\frac{1}{6}$ less than Martha.

How many charms are there in the box?

How many does each girl get?

Martha gets _____ charms.

Mimi gets _____ charms.

Mary gets _____ charms.

If the charms were divided

evenly, each girl would get

_____ charms.

Ref: Lab Sheet Annotations, page 360.   •••••••Z-10

Pat: "Father, how old are you?"

Father: "I'll tell you in a riddle:

          In ten years you will be half as old as

          I am now, but twice as old as you are now."

Pat: "Thank you for telling me.

          You are [   ] years old."

Joe: "Mother! Mother! After you took half of my

          string, Father took half of what was left and

          then brother took half of what remained and

          then sister cut that in half. How can I fly

          my kite with 60 centimeters of string?"

Question: How much string did Joe have to start with?

[   ] centimeters

or [   ] meters and △ centimeters

Ref: *Lab Sheet Annotations*, page 360.

Name _____ Date _____

Think about these questions and make good guesses. Then check your answers.

	First Guess	Answer Checked

If you walk to school . . .

about how many streets do you cross? - - - - - - - - -

about how many traffic lights do you pass? - - - - - -

about how many intersections do you pass? - - - - - -

about how many houses do you pass? - - - - - - - - -

If you ride to school . . .

about how many km away is your home? - - - - - - -

about how many traffic lights do you pass? - - - - - -

about how many turns do you make? - - - - - - - -

about how many minutes does the trip take? - - - - - -

About your school:

about how many classrooms are in your school? - - - - -

about how many children are in your school? - - - - -

about how many children under six years of age are in your school? -

about how many children over nine years of age are in your school? -

about how many books are there in your classroom? - -

about how many books are there in your school? - - - - -

about how many children in your school are boys? - - -

about how many children are absent daily in your class? (What is the average number absent daily, counted over a week?) -

Ref: *Lab Sheet Annotations*, page 361.

Name _____ Date _____

	First Guess	Answer Checked

More questions about your school:

About how many walking steps is it to the principal's office? ----

About how many meters is it to the principal's office? ------------

About how many floor tiles (or boards) are on your classroom floor?

If your classroom were empty . . .

   about how many people could sit on chairs in it? ------------

   about how many children could lie on the floor
   in it without touching each other -----------------------

   about how many children could stand up
   in it packed like sardines? ----------------------------

Questions about other things:

About how many apples are in a kilogram of apples? --------------

About how many marshmellows are there in a kilogram? ----------

About how many peanuts in a kilogram? -------------------------

About how many apples could fit in a shoe box? ----------------

About how many marshmellows in a shoe box? --------------------

About how many drops of water fill $\frac{1}{4}$ cup of water? --------------

About how many times does your heart beat in a minute? --------

About how much does a liter of milk weigh? -------------------

About how much does a liter of water weigh? ------------------

About how much does a liter of sand weigh? -------------------

About how many people live in your city? --------------------

About how many people live in your state? -------------------

About how many people live in the United States? ------------

Are there more dogs than people in the U.S.A.? ---------------   Yes   No

Are there more chickens than people in the U.S.A.? -----------   Yes   No

Ref: *Lab Sheet Annotations*, page 361.

• • • • • • Z-13